THE PRIMER FOR INSTITUTIONAL RESEARCH

edited by
Meredith A. Whiteley
John D. Porter
Robert H. Fenske

Association for Institutional Research
Resources for Institutional Research, Number Seven

Contents

This book is a primer. Like the basic texts you used in school, its purpose is to provide a "first view," or introduction, to the central issues, methods, and resources of the field. Our charge from AIR's Publications Board was to create an easy-to-use tool for new institutional researchers and others interested in the field. At the same time, we hope that *The Primer* will be a handy reference for more experienced institutional researchers.

Creating a primer that can be used by all institutional researchers is a challenge. *The Primer*'s audience differs not only in their level of experience but also in the types of environments in which they work. A quick perusal of an AIR *Directory* shows that members come from many institutional settings, including small and large, public and private colleges and universities; system offices; associations; and government offices.

Sensitivity to this diversity was a critical concern throughout the development of this book. We also tried to be sensitive to international differences. However, we are the first to admit that comparative institutional research is an area needing a great deal more work. To best meet the needs of this diverse group, we asked authors to write as generically as possible, fitting their discussions to small private colleges in rural settings as well as to large public universities in the cities. However, all chapters focus on institutional researchers in single institutions rather than multi-institutional systems or agencies. While some illustrations in specific chapters may not fit all institutional applications, the authors tried to keep their discussions of the issues and processes broad to fit most institutional settings.

In giving us direction, Publications Board members frequently referred to *The Primer* as a "cookbook" or "manual." We relied heavily on these metaphors in the conceptualization, organization, and format of *The Primer*.

Inside *The Primer*

Conceptually, the cookbook/manual concept translated into a "how-to" book designed to provide the direction institutional researchers need to start, implement, and complete specific basic projects. More theoretical or philosophic discussions of the nature and purpose of institutional research can be found in other AIR publications listed in the front of the yearly *Directory*. Presentation of emerging concepts and methodologies is the bailiwick of the *AIR Professional File*.

The tough conceptual issue was deciding what basic projects to include in this beginner's cookbook/manual for institutional research. Institutional researchers are involved in a growing range of topics and issues critical to the health of their institutions. Institutional researchers now deal frequently with not only an expanding array of more typical institutional research topics but also with information management, planning, and policy analysis. In addition, they must understand and use a growing number of paradigms from the social sciences, organizational theory, and management.

Recognizing the diversity among institutional researchers and the expanding subject matter of the field itself, our task then was to select the handful of topics that have the broadest application across the many types of institutions and that illustrate the widest range of subjects and methods institutional researchers will deal with during the next few years. Ultimately, this was a subjective and speculative call. We tried, however, to be systematic in our selection approach. We began by reviewing all of the papers presented at the annual AIR forums from 1986 through 1990. We found that the bulk of these dealt with **student** issues. Another sizable portion concerned **faculty**. Others focused more on **institutional** subjects. Still other forum papers concerned **methods**. We supplemented this review with extensive reading of the journals and monographs of the field. As we scoured the literature, we looked also for authors who went beyond the single case to draw out the more general implications of their topics.

Out of this search process, we identified eleven bread-and-butter issues we believe institutional researchers will work on during the next few years.

Three of the chapters deal with student issues. Michael Middaugh's chapter is on the continuing problem of student persistence. While Middaugh focuses his chapter on cohort survival analysis, he also looks beyond the numbers to student satisfaction surveys and analyses of the reasons students leave or persist.

Craig Clagett's chapter on enrollment management includes persistence as one of six stages in an enrollment management information needs matrix that includes performance monitoring indicators as well as broader policy research and analysis.

Jean Endo's chapter on student impacts directs you through a project using a longitudinal student impact study to analyze the impacts of a specific intervention on students. Jean includes a brief but fairly detailed guide on creating and administering surveys.

Mike McGuire and the team of Rich Howard, Julie Snyder, and Jerry McLaughlin provide direction on two key faculty analyses. Mike McGuire's chapter on faculty demand illustrates how to project your college's or university's needs for faculty. Howard, Snyder, and McLaughlin present ways of addressing the questions of salary competitiveness, compression, and equity.

The subject of the other six chapters is more institutionally oriented. Gary Hanson and Bridgett Price's chapter on academic program review lays out the process step by step, accompanied by a project description of a program review for a biology department.

Mary Ann Heverly introduces institutional researchers to total quality management and its application in colleges and universities. Heverly first presents the concepts of total quality management in comparison with the traditional management approach and then discusses its application to higher education. She concludes with a discussion of several TQM analysis methods, using graphic illustrations.

Daryl Smith provides a provocative chapter on the broad concept of diversity and analysis of how well a college or university is achieving its diversity goals. Smith shows how a shift in the focus of this analysis away from the success of individuals and toward the institution's achievement in creating an environment for success impacts research questions and types of analyses.

Jim Morrison's chapter on environmental scanning provides both an introduction to the purpose of scanning and detailed instructions on establishing a scanning process on your campus. One of the strengths of this chapter is a detailed guide to scanning resources.

Heather Haberaecker's chapter on cost analysis provides an overview of the three types of cost analyses. Heather includes a detailed example of a cost anlaysis along with a discussion of the decisions and data needed to complete a cost study.

Deb Teeter and Paul Brinkman's chapter on peer institutional comparison starts with a down-to-earth discussion of the political issues inherent in peer selection. Teeter and Brinkman then explain the different types of comparison and several of the peer selection methodologies.

Incorporated in these eleven chapters are discussions and illustrations of a wide spectrum of methods, including quantitative approaches, such as regression analysis, and qualitative approaches, such as focus groups. The chapter on faculty salaries by Snyder, McLaughlin, and Howard, for example, discusses the use of regression to analyze salary equity and directs you to a few key references on both the variables to consider and more detailed explication of the methodology. Craig Clagett's chapter on enrollment management includes a sidebar discussion of focus groups. Mike McGuire's chapter on faculty demand also uses a sidebar to present interactive modeling.

The cookbook/manual concept influenced the organization of the chapters in *The Primer* by demanding that each stand alone. This means you do not have to read *The Primer* from cover to cover to be able to use it. Nor do chapters and concepts build from simple to complex. Instead, *The Primer* is designed to be used over and over again, as you need it. If today you need help with enrollment management, turn to Craig Clagett's chapter. Next month or next year, when pressure builds for you to initiate environmental scanning or a total quality management approach, you will want to pull out your dog-eared copy of *The Primer* again.

Cookbooks and manuals usually also have a high degree of structural consistency. Following this example, all the chapters in *The Primer* begin with a discussion of the central issues you must understand in working on the topic. With just a few exceptions, each chapter then progresses through a background literature section to discussion of the data, analysis, and communication issues specific to the topic. Each chapter closes with a brief "remember," recapping the central points and sometimes raising an important warning to consider before you launch into your project.We editorially modified each author's manuscript to fit within *The Primer*'s format.

In addition, we used a number of graphic format features to provide illustration and make the chapters more readily usable. We included sidebars in a number of chapters to keep the chapters focused and yet provide the maximum illustration and direction. In some chapters, like those on faculty demand and persistence, the sidebars are separate presentations of methods. In Mary Ann Heverly's chapter on total quality management, the sidebar outlines the actual implementation of the approach at Delaware County Community College.

The eleven chapters are illustrated by tables, models, and figures. In some cases, these graphics show how you might display your data. In others, the graphics lay out the components of the process or help you visualize its steps. In all of the examples, the authors try to teach through example the importance of simple and clear graphics.

Perhaps the most radical feature of *The Primer* is the shaded reference boxes scattered throughout the chapters. The purpose of the references listed in these eleven chapters is to provide you with a starting place, not to provide a history of the literature or theoretical development. In keeping with this focus, we asked authors to cite just a few of the most recent overviews of the subject and methods. Jim Morrison's chapter on environmental scanning is an exception to this rule. In this chapter, Morrison provides a guide to the periodicals you might consider in establishing a scanning process.

We believe that in addition to being up-to-date and focused, it is important that every reference cited in *The Primer* be generally accessible to institutional researchers in every type of institutional setting. To ensure this accessibility, we provide either the ERIC Document Reproduction Service accession number or the address (and usually the phone number) for ordering every paper, monograph, and report cited. Of course, as time passes, these will become increasingly outdated. See our "Editors' Note" on the first page of Jim Morrison's chapter for general guidance on how to obtain more up-to-date ordering information for all of the citations included in *The Primer*.

As you well know, a project the size of this Prim*er* is always highly cooperative. We thank our great group of authors for their flexibility, patience, and high degree of commitment to their colleagues around the world. We also thank Arizona State University for its professional support of the Association for Institutional Research through this project. Most importantly, we credit the people behind the scenes: Nancy Dickson for her graphic expertise, Melinda Gebel for her copy editing, Kathleen Wolk for ensuring that the references are complete and accessible, and Rita Hillis for her patience and professionalism in creating every line and graphic of *The Primer for Institutional Research*.

Meredith A. Whiteley
John D. Porter
Robert H. Fenske
Tempe, Arizona
June, 1992

About the Editors

Meredith A. Whiteley *is senior research analyst in the Office of Institutional Analysis at Arizona State University. She attended Grinnell College and holds a master's degree in history and a Ph.D. in higher education from Arizona State University. Meredith is secretary of the Society for College and University Planning's Publications Advisory Board and president of University Career Women at Arizona State. She has written on scenarios and futures planning, demographic analysis, and peers.*

John D. Porter *is director of the Office of Institutional Analysis at Arizona State University. He holds a master's degree in business administration from the University of Utah and a Ph.D. in higher education from Arizona State University. John is a Certified Public Accountant in Arizona. He has written on scenarios and futures planning and student financial aid.*

Robert H. Fenske *is professor of higher education at Arizona State University. He earned both a master's degree and Ph.D. from the University of Wisconsin. Bob is a charter member of AIR and received AIR's Outstanding Service Award in 1982. His most recent research is in the area of student aid.*

Persistence

Michael F. Middaugh

ISSUES

Most Americans still think that college students go directly from high school to college and four years later leave college with the coveted baccalaureate in hand. Reality, however, is more accurately depicted in the February 1990 *Chronicle of Higher Education* headline: "Only 15% of students graduate in four years, a new study finds" (February 21, 1990, p. 1).

How the patterns of persistence and attrition play out in your institution is a critical issue. The optimal size of your student body is predicated upon classroom capacity and existing faculty resources. The number of new students admitted to your institution each year is a function of what proportion of each entering cohort actually complete a degree and how long it takes them to do it.

To address these issues, you will be asked to provide answers to questions such as:

- What proportion of students who enter your college or university as matriculants in an academic program actually

Enrollment planning and resource management depend upon your ability as an institutional researcher to accurately measure persistence and attrition.

receive a degree at your institution?

- How long does it take, on average, for students to complete a degree?

- What proportion of students leave without graduating?

- At what point in their academic careers do these students leave? After one semester? Two semesters? Three or more semesters?

- What are the underlying reasons associated with student persistence and attrition at your college or university?

Enrollment planning and resource management depend upon your ability as an institutional researcher to accurately measure persistence and attrition. Imprecise measurement of persistence and attrition can result in overcrowded or underutilized classrooms, excessive student faculty ratios, or inefficient use of faculty resources. Further, there is mounting pressure from outside the

Michael F. Middaugh is the director of Institutional Research and Planning at the University of Delaware. He is also past president of the North East Association for Institutional Research.

institution for information on persistence, attrition, and graduation rates. Public Law 101-542, known as the Student Right to Know Act and signed into law on November 8, 1990, requires colleges and universities to publish the proportion of their first-time freshmen who graduate within six years. A parallel reporting requirement from the National Collegiate Athletic Association (NCAA) requires public disclosure of graduation rates for student athletes. Institutional and professional accreditation agencies, other external agencies, and the media similarly request data on persistence and graduation rates.

This chapter is a "how to" approach that will help you begin to collect information immediately. The chapter provides you with background information and some concrete strategies for conducting research on student persistence and attrition. Books and journals cited as a literature base in the following pages are but a sampling of the resources available that will help you get started. The methodologies described in this chapter will provide you with a strong base for developing a customized research program appropriate to the information needs of your institution.

BACKGROUND

Since attrition is most likely to occur between the first and second fall semesters in a student's career, a basic understanding of the dynamics of a student's first year of higher education is essen-

tial. *The Freshman Year Experience* (Upcraft & Gardner, 1989) is an excellent start. Another group of literature discusses how the "fit" between individual student needs and the characteristics of a college or university (e.g., size, quality, accessibility of faculty, academic and social support systems) is a major factor in determining whether students leave an institution or stay and complete the degree.

Institutional researchers can play a major role in quantifying the college experience as it relates to the phenomenon of student persistence and attrition. Read the resource materials cited in this section with an eye toward how the information relates to your institution. Think of the variables in the studies, the data collection

---

For studies of factors affecting student/college fit, see:

Tinto, V. (1987). *Leaving college: Rethinking the causes and cures of student attrition*. Chicago: University of Chicago Press.

Upcraft, M.L., & Gardner, J.N. (1989). *The freshman year experience*. San Francisco: Jossey-Bass.

Pascarella, E.T., & Terenzini, P.T. (1991). *How college affects students*. San Francisco: Jossey-Bass.

---

strategies employed, and the implications drawn from the analyses as tools that you can use for better student persistence and attrition within your own institutional context. Also, use the references to other literature contained in these resources to further your understanding of persistence and attrition.

For examples of persistence data presentations, see:

Porter, O.F. (1989). *Undergraduate completion and persistence at four-year colleges and universities: Completers, persisters, stopouts, and dropouts.* National Institute of Independent Colleges and Universities, Ste. 750, 122 C St., NW, Washington, DC 20001.

Middaugh, M.F. (1990). *A handbook for newcomers to institutional research.* North East Association for Institutional Research, c/o University of Delaware, Newark, DE 19716.

Noel, L., Levitz, R., Saluri, D., & Associates. (1986). *Increasing student retention.* San Francisco: Jossey-Bass.

DATA

As you start collecting data, it is helpful to see how others assemble and present data. Noel, Levitz, Saluri and Associates' (1986) review of the national student retention data is an excellent example of how to assemble and present data. It is useful also to have a source-book available that presents concrete analytical strategies for massaging data of various types once they have been collected.

Cohort Survival Analysis

The immediate task at hand is to determine persistence, attrition, and graduation rates. The tool of choice for most institutional researchers is *cohort survival analysis*. This technique examines discrete cohorts of students over time and compares the headcounts at initial point of entry into the institution with the headcounts at regular intervals (usually at the beginning of each fall semester) to determine the number within each cohort who remain at the institution (persistence or retention),

the number who graduate, and the number who withdraw from the institution without receiving a degree (attrition).

In embarking on a cohort survival analysis, it is important to define exactly who is in the cohort at the outset and to keep the cohort homogeneously consistent throughout the analysis. For example, it is imprecise to only study transition rates from freshman to sophomore year, sophomore to junior year, and junior to senior year. Students who enter your institution as first-time students (i.e., have never attended another college) may leave at some point before their senior year and be replaced by a student transferring to your school from another institution. The overall headcount would remain the same, while actual persistence and attrition activity would be masked.

At the University of Delaware, we look at cohort survival for first-time freshmen and for transfer students separately. It makes sense to analyze data in that manner because the institution serves students largely within the traditional 18- to 22-year-old college-going age group. Community colleges might wish to take a different view. For example, first-time freshmen and returning adult students might be key cohorts for analysis. Comprehensive colleges with large continuing education efforts might wish to look at the continuing education cohort as a separate entity. Your college or university should determine which student types or groupings it wishes to analyze. The important points here are the following:

- The cohort should be defined with precision.

- The cohort should have integrity at its inception, that is, be uniform with respect to its composition (e.g., first-time freshmen, transfer students).

- Cohort members should be consistent throughout the analysis (i.e., no additions after initial definition of the cohort).

As noted earlier, cohort survival implies headcount comparisons within a given cohort at regular intervals over an extended period of time. Official fall term enrollments are the traditional checkpoint at most institutions.

It is important for the comparability of data that the same point in time be used for each term under analysis. Some institutions use the date, usually in late September or early October, on which campus databases are "frozen" for reporting purposes; that is, extracts from the databases are created for use in all subsequent reporting activity. Other institutions use end-of-term (late December) data. Students come and go at an institution throughout a term, and data on students taken at different points in the term rarely match. Therefore, it is important to be consistent once you have chosen the times in a given term at which you examine student data from year to year. The length of time for monitoring activity within a cohort has been historically a matter of institutional choice. However,

recent federal reporting requirements under the Student Right to Know Act mandate the analysis of student persistence and graduation rates over a minimum of six years, or 12 consecutive traditional semesters.

Table 1 illustrates the concept of cohort survival analysis employing data from the University of Delaware. Using an electronic spreadsheet, the table lists six separate freshman cohorts with the years in which each entered the university as first-time students. The number of first-time freshmen in the entering cohort is displayed in the column headed "1st Fall," and the number in the cohort who persist or graduate are displayed under subsequent headings. By dividing the number of persisters by the total number in the original cohort, a persistence rate is calculated and is displayed as "% enrollment." Subtracting the persistence rate from 100 results in an attrition rate, which is displayed as "% dropout" in the table. Persistence rates are displayed for each fall semester following the initial semester of entry for a period of six years. Graduation rates are displayed separately.

To illustrate, of the 3,121 first-time freshmen entering in fall 1985, 2,632 or 84.3 percent persisted into the sophomore year; 15.7 percent were lost to attrition during the same time frame. **Table 1** shows comparable persistence and attrition calculations for the five subsequent cohorts. The graduation rate for the fall 1985 cohort

Table 1

Enrollments, Persistence Rates, and Graduation Rates for First-time Freshmen University Total

				Enrollment and Dropout Rates			Graduation Rates	
Entering Fall Term	1st Fall	2nd Fall	3rd Fall	4th Fall	5th Fall	6th+ Fall	within 4 yrs	within 5 yrs
1985 N	3121	2632	2382	2291	768	139	1367	2061
% enrollment	100.0	84.3	76.3	73.4	24.6	4.5	43.8	66.0
% dropout	0.0	15.7	23.7	26.3	31.6	29.5		
1986 N	3313	2842	2575	2483	802	120	1495	2231
% enrollment	100.0	85.8	77.7	74.9	24.2	3.6	45.1	67.3
% dropout	0.0	14.2	22.3	24.8	30.7	29.0		
1987 N	3168	2764	2484	2397	708	0	1505	—
% enrollment	100.0	87.2	78.4	75.7	22.3	0.0	47.5	
% dropout	0.0	12.8	21.6	24.0	30.1	0.0		
1988 N	3301	2848	2598	2509	0	0	—	—
% enrollment	100.0	86.3	78.7	76.0	0.0	0.0		
% dropout	0.0	13.7	21.3	23.6	0.0	0.0		
1989 N	2917	2508	2271	0	0	0	—	—
% enrollment	100.0	86.0	77.9	0.0	0.0	0.0		
% dropout	0.0	14.0	22.2	0.0	0.0	0.0		
1990 N	2947	2473	0	0	0	0	—	—
% enrollment	100.0	83.9	0.0	0.0	0.0	0.0		
% dropout	0.0	16.1	0.0	0.0	0.0	0.0		

finished at 66.0 percent, the 1986 cohort at 67.3 percent. The table further demonstrates that for the period under analysis, just under one-half of entering freshmen graduate within four years, while two of every three entering freshmen secure their degree within five years.

The process for tracking students over time is quite simple. Students generally are assigned an identi-fication number at the time they initially register at a college or university. Where the same student identification number in the student records database shows active course registration in semesters subsequent to that of initial registration, the student clearly is persisting. Where a student shows active course registration in a given fall semester but none the following fall semester, and no graduation flag is associated with that student identification number in the database, it is possible that the student left the institution, becoming an attrition statistic.

It is important to point out that persistence and attrition rates can fluctuate within a given cohort over time, as evidenced in **Table 1**. This is particularly common in colleges and universities serving significant numbers of nontraditional students (e.g., returning adult students, students holding full-time jobs, part-time students). It is not uncommon for these students to "stop-out," that is, take one or more semesters off from study to work, travel, or attend to family matters, only to subsequently return and resume study. Most institutions have established time limits for stopping out. At the University of Delaware, given the traditional nature of the student body, if a student fails to register for coursework for three consecutive semesters, it is assumed that he or she has permanently withdrawn from the institution and that individual is no longer included in the cohort. You may wish to establish different parameters for defining stopping out at your institution. As with all other phases of cohort survival analysis, be consistent.

The format used in displaying the data in **Table 1** can be used in further analyzing persistence, attrition, and graduation patterns among specific segments of entering cohorts. Using any of the readily available, commercially prepared statistical software packages, student identification numbers can be segmented on the basis of other demographic variables associated with the identification number in the student records database (e.g., gender, race/ethnicity, geographic residence, student major), thereby permitting development of persistence and graduation rates for any characteristic of interest to the institution. These data are extremely useful in communicating information about selected groups of students to various campus special interest constituencies.

A word about the software used in cohort survival analysis: Most institutions have computerized student records systems against which statistical software packages and electronic spreadsheets can be run to facilitate the analyses just described. The newcomer to institutional research should talk to colleagues in other institutions similar to his or her own with respect to size and available resources. Those colleagues can steer you to specific software packages that might be appropriate to your institution. Similarly, attending AIR and regional institutional research association meetings provide you other opportunities for identifying tools appropriate to your institution's size and budget to aid in cohort survival analysis.

ANALYSIS

Data from cohort survival analyses are essential to informing your institution about the extent to which it is graduating the students it recruited as first-time freshmen or as transfer students. The data are also essential to solid enrollment planning.

Student Flow

As mentioned earlier, stable persistence and attrition rates permit enrollment planners to arrive at reasonable estimates of the number of entering freshmen in a given cohort who are likely to remain at the institution until graduation and the length of time

---

For discussions and methodologies of enrollment projections, see:

Weiler, W.C. (1980). A model for short-term institutional enrollment forecasting. *Journal of Higher Education, 51*(3), 314-327.

Dickey, A.K., Asher, J.A., & Tweddale, R.B. (1989). Projecting headcount and credit hour enrollment by age group, gender, and degree level. *Research in Higher Education, 30* (1), 1-19.

---

that it will take to get there. This information is critical to academic planning; it assists in determining where faculty should be hired, the number of course sections that should be offered, etc. It also is essential to programming student services and to accurately estimating the tuition revenues needed to underwrite institutional activity.

Returning to **Table 1**, by reading the columns in the table from top to bottom, trend data with respect to persistence and attrition patterns are available for each of the four years, five years, six years or beyond that members of a cohort move through an institution. By examining these data systematically and averaging them in a

sensible fashion, you can develop basic persistence, attrition, and transitional (movement from one student level to the next) coefficients to construct a basic student flow model. It is then possible to project enrollments into the future by applying these coefficients to cohorts by varying hypothetical sizes in the outlying years. Refined projections should become increasingly accurate over time. The extent to which you can accurately estimate student enrollment will enhance the quality of revenue forecasts, staffing projections, and other essential planning tools.

Beyond the Numbers

Cohort survival and student flow analyses are extremely useful tools for defining student persistence, attrition, and graduation rates and for estimating student enrollments into the future. However, these tools do not explore the underlying reasons why students choose to leave a college or university or stay until they graduate. To address this issue, most institutions turn to some form of survey research. There are essentially two strategies for approaching this type of research.

Student Satisfaction Survey Resources:

American College Testing Program
P.O. Box 168
Iowa City, IA 52243

The College Board
45 Columbus Avenue
New York, NY 10023

National Center for Higher Education Management Systems (NCHEMS)
P.O. Drawer P
Boulder, CO 90302

The first is to administer a withdrawing student survey to those students who have left your institution without graduating. A second approach is to statistically massage the data collected from student satisfaction surveys. The American College Testing Program, The College Board, and the National Center for Higher Education Management Systems (NCHEMS) all produce data collection instruments for both withdrawing student and student satisfaction analyses. This discussion will consider each approach, and you and your colleagues should determine which is best for your institution.

Withdrawing student surveys are developed to assess which, if any, areas of student programs and services at a given institution fall short of a student's needs. They further probe to determine whether personal circumstances (i.e., illness, financial difficulties, or family situation) contributed to the student's decision to withdraw. The surveys also generally ask if the student intends to return to that college or university. In short, these data collection tools are targeted specifically at those students who leave a postsecondary institution without graduating and key their questions precisely on those variables that research has demonstrated to be specific contributors to student attrition. The difficulty with withdrawing student surveys is that they have notoriously low response rates.

In most instances, students leave the institution with no intention of returning; consequently, these students have absolutely no vested interest in responding to these surveys. While follow-up techniques in the survey administration may improve the response rate by a few percentage points, it is not uncommon to see response rates in the 20 to 35 percent range. Thus, to get a critical mass of respondents of sufficient size so that your analysis will carry weight among the campus skeptics, your survey sample has to be fairly large. This factor can result in significant expense.

An alternative strategy to withdrawing student surveys is that of statistical manipulation of data from student satisfaction surveys. Most colleges and universities have a basic program of institutional research, frequently as part of their ongoing reaccreditation activity, through which they regularly and systemically survey students to assess their satisfaction with programs, services, and other aspects of student life at the institution.

If the institutional research office is involved at the outset in the study of student satisfaction levels, it is possible to make certain that the study sample is representative of the larger student body. By asking students to voluntarily supply their student identification number on the survey so that extended research can be performed, and having assured the students of the confidentiality of their responses, it is then possible to again use the student satisfaction survey results at a later point in time. For example, having administered the survey in the spring semester, it is possible the following fall, through use of student identification numbers, to segment the population into those students returning for fall study and those students failing to return and who did not graduate. Statistical tests can then be performed to determine where significant differences may exist between persisting and withdrawing students on each of the satisfaction dimensions.

The advantage to using the student satisfaction analysis approach to assess the underlying reasons why a student withdraws is that the responses tend to be candid and are captured at the point where the student's dissatisfaction is still fresh. The likelihood is also high that a significant number of soon-to-be withdrawing students will fall within the respondent pool, as response rates of 60 to 70 percent to these surveys are not uncommon. At the same time, the researcher must infer that the areas of dissatisfaction are the contributing reasons in the student's decision to withdraw. For example, strong dissatisfaction with institutional financial aid policies may imply that the respondent was in financial distress and/or did not qualify for sufficient student aid. On the other hand, although response rates can be problematic, withdrawing student surveys pose direct questions that enable the researcher to say unequivocally that the respondent indicated that financial aid or some other variable(s) led to the decision to withdraw. You, as an institutional researcher, must weigh the advantages and disadvantages of each strategy and select the approach that best meets your information needs.

An extremely useful, albeit time-consuming, approach to enriching data on why students leave an institution without graduating is the structured exit interview, generally administered at the time a student applies for formal withdrawal from an institution. The interview is an opportunity for personal contact with the student and a chance to probe in some detail the underlying reasons for withdrawal. The difficulty is that most withdrawing students do not go through a formal process; they simply do not return to the institution. Some schools adopt a strategy wherein when a registrar's office receives a request for a transcript from a student who is not graduating, the request is viewed as a potential signal that a transfer from the institution is imminent. The student then may be contacted to determine whether this is, in fact, the case and if circumstances at the institution contributed to the decision to attend elsewhere.

When institutional researchers successfully collect valid and usable data that clarifies why some students persist while others leave, the information contributes significantly to both academic and student service program planning. As suggested by the literature, research has clearly established that the "fit" between student aspirations and needs and the range of programs and services which a college or university offers is a major force in student persistence. As the primary data collection arm of your institution, you can provide valuable information directed at enhancing that "fit."

COMMUNICATION

You now have a fuller appreciation for the basic components of research into student persistence and attrition. Having collected the data, how can you communicate the results in a way that will be most helpful to your campus? Consider the following:

- *Share the data on persistence, attrition, and graduation rates* with senior campus managers and, particularly, with deans and department chairs. Invite their suggestions on which groups of students should be examined through cohort survival analysis as a component of better understanding student flow at your institution. Not every school can have a 90 percent graduation rate. Use the data to stimulate discussion on whether your persistence and graduation rates are consistent with the specific mission of your college or university. A simulation showing budget and staff implications of a 10 percent increase or decrease in retention lends a dramatic impact.

- *Use comparative data that becomes available as the result of the Student Right to Know Act* to examine your graduation rate against that of other institutions. Be sure, however, that you are certain common definitions were used among you and your comparators in collecting the data. Use these comparisons to stimulate discussion as to the optimal institutional graduation rate in light of your school's mission.

- *Use student flow data to initiate planning discussions* on what size your student body should be in the year 2000. If that goal is to be achieved, how will that affect the number of new students you must recruit? How will improving your persistence and graduation rates specifically impact the number of new students you must recruit in an increasingly competitive admissions marketplace? How will these numbers affect revenue projections and faculty demand? Position yourself to be the quantitative arm of the campus planning process.

- *Use the data collected from your student surveys to find the underlying reasons for persistence and attrition* as tools to help campus planners focus on areas of student satisfaction as well as dissatisfaction. This will assist you in sharpening the "fit" between what your institution offers and the needs of your clientele. This, in turn, should lead to improved persistence and graduation rates.

REMEMBER

Above all, be creative in your approaches to research on student persistence and attrition. This chapter is intended to whet your appetite and get you started. It is hardly an exhaustive treatment of the subject. Continue to read and to think about the issues discussed in the preceding pages. Take these baseline strategies and refine and improve them to make them more responsive to your institution's specific needs. And above all, share your strategies and results with your colleagues in the institutional research profession through participation in regional association meetings, especially at the annual AIR forum. Good luck!

Enrollment Management

Craig Clagett

ISSUES

Enrollment management is the coordinated effort of a college or university to influence the size and characteristics of the institution's student body. Enrollment is "managed" through a variety of strategies, including admissions, pricing, financial aid, and advising. Well-designed and well-executed institutional research is the key to successful enrollment management.

Conceptually, enrollment management links research on individual college choice, student-institution fit, and retention. Before addressing institutional policy issues affecting the size and characteristics of the student body, managers need to understand the forces that influence choice, fit, and retention on their campus. To do so, enrollment managers need answers to numerous questions concerning each stage of a student's experience with the institution, including the following:

• *Inquiry.* How widely known is the college? How do prospective students view the college? What other institutions are considered by prospective students?

• *Application.* How can we increase the size of the applicant pool? How can we attract the students we would most like to enroll?

• *Enrollment.* How can we improve yield? How effective are our existing recruitment activities? What factors differentiate our college from its closest competitors and influence admitted students' final choices?

• *Persistence.* What influence does financial aid have on student decisions to enroll and persist? What is the perceived campus culture or climate, and what influence do these factors have on retention and attrition?

• *Completion.* What proportion of a freshman class persists to graduation? Do any student subgroups exhibit significantly higher than average attrition? Why do some students persist while others do not?

• *Alumni.* How successful are our alumni in their postgraduate endeavors? What proportion remains involved with the institution? What characteristics describe alumni donors?

Craig Clagett is the director of Institutional Research and Analysis at Prince George's Community College in Largo, Maryland. He served as president of Maryland AIR and is a two-time contributor to the AIR Professional File.

This sampling of student decision and institutional policy questions captures the comprehensive, long-range nature of an enrollment management plan. It is important to remember that the results of recruitment are measured not just in terms of the number and characteristics of new students who enroll but also by the number who become well-adapted, successful students and productive alumni.

The encompassing reach of enrollment management suggests the difficulty in implementing a successful enrollment management program. Larger universities, where enrollment management responsibilities may be widely dispersed, pose particularly challenging tasks of coord-

ination and monitoring. Indeed, Dolence (1989-90) asserts that over one half of the institutions that try to establish enrollment management programs fail.

Institutional researchers provide the link between these microlevel analyses and enrollment management policy development. One useful method for analyzing student enrollment is the linear student flow model. This linear model tracks the student from initial preapplication inquiry through application, enrollment, completion, and postgraduation follow-up. This chapter provides the basics on how to design and conduct linear student flow analysis and interpret the results into useful policy implications for enrollment management.

BACKGROUND

The literature pertinent to enrollment management falls into two broad types. The first is the recent work explicitly concerning enrollment management as an organizational construct or process. Written within the past 10 years, this literature is largely responsible for the spread of the concept and language of enrollment management. The second, and more diverse, body of literature consists of the research and policy studies that form the necessary information infrastructure supporting the successful implementation of an enrollment management process. Research into student college choice, student-institution fit, pricing and financial aid, student

---

For literature on enrollment management as an organizational construct, see:

Kemerer, F.R., Baldridge, V.J., & Green, K.C. (1982). *Strategies for effective enrollment management*. American Association of State Colleges and Universities, One DuPont Circle, NW, Ste. 700, Washington, DC 20036. Phone: 202/293-7070.

Hossler, D. (Ed.). (1986). Managing college enrollments. *New Directions for Higher Education, 53*. San Francisco: Jossey-Bass.

Hossler, D. (1987). *Creating effective enrollment management systems*. College Entrance Examination Board, 45 Columbus Avenue, New York, NY. Phone: 212/713-8000.

Dolence, M.G., Miyahara, D.H., Grajeda, J., & Rapp, C. (1987-88). Strategic enrollment management and planning. *Planning for Higher Education, 16*(3), 55-74.

Dolence, M.G. (1989-90). Evaluation criteria for an enrollment management program. *Planning for Higher Education, 18*(1), 1-13.

---

attrition, and other related topics can all be considered part of this second group of enrollment management-related literature.

Organizational Construct

Since enrollment management requires the integration of several institutional functions, much of the early enrollment management literature focused on organizational structures. Don Hossler's prolific writings contributed to the expanding use of the phrase "enrollment management," if not its actualization. Another good source is Kemerer, Baldridge, and Green (1982). They identified four separate enrollment management models characterized by varying degrees of administrative support or centralization.

Surveys conducted in the 1980s showed that approximately two thirds of responding campuses had some sort of enrollment management program in place; however, the literature also suggested that effective programs were rare. In fact, in many instances, "enrollment management" was simply a new term for the work of admissions offices. Would-be "enrollment managers" were not developing the requisite knowledge base in student college choice, student-institution fit, student retention and attrition, and impact of financial aid but were changing titles and rearranging organizational charts.

Research and Policy Studies

A growing body of literature provides enrollment managers

with a foundation for interpreting their own campus research and experience. The literature listed here provides a starting place on the subject. Each contains more extensive bibliographies to guide further study.

In addition to the findings of educational research found in the literature, the institutional researcher relies heavily on institution-specific information. Useful articles include Davis-Van Atta and Carrier (in Hossler, 1986) and Glover (1986).

> **For help interpreting your campus experience, see:**
>
> Glover, R.H. (1986). Designing a decision-support system for enrollment management. *Research in Higher Education, 24*(1), 15-34.
>
> Lay, R.S., & Endo, J.J. (Eds.). (1987). Designing and using market research. *New Directions for Institutional Research, 54.* San Francisco: Jossey-Bass.
>
> Leslie, L.L., & Brinkman, P.T. (1987). Student price response in higher education. *Journal of Higher Education, 58*(2), 181-203.
>
> Tinto, V. (1987). *Leaving college: Rethinking the causes and cures of student attrition.* Chicago: University of Chicago Press.
>
> Fenske, R.H. (Ed.). (1989). Studying the impact of student aid on institutions. *New Directions for Institutional Research, 62.* San Francisco: Jossey-Bass.
>
> Hossler, D. (Ed.). (1991). Evaluating student recruitment and retention programs. *New Directions for Institutional Research, 70.* San Franciso: Jossey-Bass.

DATA

The enrollment manager needs two different types of information: **performance monitoring indicators** (PMIs) and **policy research and analysis**. PMIs are specific quantifiable measures used to

Figure 1						
Enrollment Management Information Needs Matrix						
	← RECRUITMENT				RETENTION →	
	Inquiry	Application	Enrollment	Persistence	Completion	Alumni
Performance Monitoring Indicators (PMIs)						
Policy Research and Analysis						

track and evaluate the implementation and success of an enrollment management program. Ideally, PMIs are developed with the consultation of the offices responsible for each stage of the enrollment process and are used by the enrollment manager to evaluate the performance of each unit as well as to oversee the broader institutional enrollment picture. Policy research and analysis, on the other hand, is conducted to assist unit directors and the enrollment management planning team in developing strategies for achieving the goals associated with the PMIs.

Figure 1 summarizes the information needs of the enrollment management process. This process is divided into two phases: **recruitment** and **retention**. Each phase has three distinct stages that generate information needs. In recruitment, the stages are: *inquiry, application,* and *enrollment.* In retention, the stages are: *persistence, completion,* and *alumni.* PMIs are needed at all six of the stages of a student's experience with the institution.

Performance Monitoring Indicators (PMIs)

PMIs typically are simple counts or ratios that report the status of enrollment at a point in time. **Figure 2** shows examples of PMIs for the recruitment phase, encompassing each of the three stages (i.e., inquiry, application, and enrollment). During these stages, indicators may be followed closely. Indeed, key PMIs, such as applications, acceptances, and paid and unpaid registrations, may be tracked daily during application and enrollment. A separate management report tracking enrollment in individual courses might be updated daily during the last two weeks of registration to guide academic administrators in course decisions and faculty assignments.

The enrollment management plan should delineate which PMIs are to be tracked and specify targets for each. At the minimum, the

Figure 2

Recruitment

Performance Monitoring Indicators (PMIs)	
Inquiry	Number of mail and phone inquiries
Application	Number of applications received
	Number of acceptances offered
	Percent of applicants offered admission
	Number of accepted applicants enrolling
	Percent of accepted applicants enrolling
Enrollment	Full-time equivalent enrollment
	Student average courseload
	Number of full- and part-time first-time freshmen
	Number of new transfer students
	Number of exceptional and conditional admits
	Number, type, and amount of financial aid awards
	Share of local area residents/high school grads enrolling
	Racial/ethnic composition of entering students
	Mean/distribution of SAT scores
	High school GPA/rank distributions of entering students
	Predicted freshman academic performance
	Number and percent of entering students needing remediation
	Distribution of enrollment by college and program
	Distribution of enrollment by class location and time

enrollment management team needs clear expectations about the number of applicants, offers of admission, and resulting anticipated enrollees. Other important PMIs include the full/part-time ratio, total credit hours enrolled, and full-time equivalent students. Since enrollment management concerns the characteristics as well as the magnitude of enrollment, other attributes, such as the SAT score distribution of applications, admits, and enrollees, may be monitored as well. Usually the racial/ethnic composition at each stage is reported to help in achieving student diversity goals. For departmental planning, the distribution of enrollments by college, program, discipline, class location, and time are important PMIs.

Performance monitoring indicators also are needed for the retention phase, including not only persistence to completion but also the student's association with the

Figure 3

Retention

Performance Monitoring Indicators (PMIs)	
Persistence	2nd-semester retention rates of student subgroups
	Persistence rates to sophomore, junior, and senior status
Completion	Graduation rates for subgroups
Alumni	Number in graduating class entering graduate school
	Number passing licensure
	Percentage obtaining program-related employment in first year after graduation
	Percentage satisfied with college experience
	Number making contributions

institution as an alumnus. **Figure 3** lists some of the important PMIs for assessing stages in this phase.

The data for monitoring the enrollment management effort comes from student applications and registration transactions. The typical campus student information system contains both term enrollment and transcript files that include demographic, course enrollment, and performance data useful for enrollment monitoring purposes.

Special record-keeping procedures may need to be implemented. For example, you may need a way to track mail and phone inquiries. Other methods are needed to gather background information not contained in your college's application form, such as high school study habits or parents' educational attainment. This is particularly likely for community colleges that often use an abbreviated application form. In addition, a method of collecting data

on students' use of such services is needed to evaluate academic support services, such as tutoring or mentoring programs.

Policy Research and Analysis

The data needed for policy research and analysis depend on the particular policy issue. Data from the student information system are necessary but frequently not sufficient. This area of enrollment management research requires surveys, focus groups, and peer institution data collection. Standardized questionnaires, peer analyses, and market research are available from commercial enterprises as an alternative to supplement institutionally designed studies.

Organizing the Data

Organizing enrollment management data for effective use often is more difficult than collecting it. Both standard transcript files and term files pose a number of

17

For information on focus groups, see:

Goldman, A.E., & McDonald, S.S. (1987). *The group depth interview: Its principles and practice.* Englewood Cliffs, NJ: Prentice Hall.

For discussion of focus groups in institutional research:

Bers, T.H. (1987). Exploring institutional images through focus group interviews. In R.S. Lay & J.J. Endo (Eds.). Designing and using market research. *New Directions for Institutional Research, 54,* 19-29. San Francisco: Jossey-Bass.

problems when they are used for student flow studies. Many transcript file systems overwrite old data with new, destroying the historical record critical for student flow analysis. Term file systems, on the other hand, keep the data intact. However, these files are frequently stored off-line, requiring programming and manipulation before being used in analysis.

Data from surveys provide another set of challenges. Survey research often is conducted separately, with little or no consideration given to the interrelationship between variables and institutional data sets. Integrating the two requires careful attention to the details of student identification, variable definitions, representation, and sample bias.

The effective application of data analysis to enrollment management decision-making is helped

Figure 4
Sample Data Elements for Student Tracking System

Student Attributes at Entry	
Sudent ID number (SSN)	Admissions/placement test scores
Date of birth	Prior college attended/transfer credits
Gender	Financial aid need/award type and level
Race/ethnicity	Reason for attending/goal at this institution
Native language	Program of study
High school attended/class rank and GPA	Resident/commuter status
Student Progress Term-by-Term	
Remediation attempted and completed	Program of study
Credit hours attempted and earned this term	Cumulative credits attempted and earned at end of term
Term grade point average	Cumulative GPA at end of term
Academic standing	Degree or certificate awarded
Follow-up Indicators, Graduates and Leavers	
Transfer/graduate school	Relationship of job to college program
Credits accepted/lost in transfer	Annual salary
Transfer/graduate school program	Employer/industry and location
Cumulative credits earned/GPA at transfer school	Employer ratings of student job preparation
Degree awarded/program of degree	Alumni association/fund donor
Employment status	

Focus Groups

Focus group interviewing is especially appropriate for understanding why students make the enrollment decisions they do. In a focus group, a trained moderator facilitates an informal discussion, lasting approximately 90 minutes, among 8 to 12 participants. Discussion focuses on one or two key questions identified by the project sponsors. Focus group research requires rigorous preparation and careful analysis.

Developing Research Questions. Research questions may evolve from conversations with administrators, from tracking systems data, or other quantitative research. The moderator provides a loose structure to direct questioning, using exploratory questions, followed by probes, to elicit more in-depth elaboration. Sensitive issues should be introduced near the end of the session.

Selecting Group Participants. Participants are selected from groups with characteristics appropriate to the purpose and goals of the project. Since it is always possible that an atypical group may be selected, more than one focus group should be conducted on each topic. Monetary incentives are usually needed to ensure attendance.

Selecting the Moderator. A skilled moderator is essential. The moderator should be a person who can establish a good rapport with participants by drawing out reticent participants, by preventing strong personalities from dominating the discussion, and by ensuring a fair hearing for all opinions while maintaining the group's focus. It is best if the moderator is someone other than the research sponsor. An independent, trained moderator probably will be more successful in maintaining objectivity. The moderator should have enough knowledge of the project to be able to recognize and follow up on pertinent comments.

Conducting the Analysis. Rather than attempting to quantify the extent to which attitudes are held in the population, focus group findings are used to identify themes and to develop insights into the opinions behind behavior. Analysts must be careful not to give undue attention to the views of the more articulate members of the group.

by paying attention to these four principles:

- *Construct freestanding longitudinal tracking files.* Instead of using discrete files established for other purposes, construct separate longitudinal cohort tracking files. These freestanding files facilitate analysis by paralleling the student flow continuum from inquiry to postgraduation by preserving key data values. **Figure 4** displays data elements commonly included in these longitudinal files.

  In addition to determining which data elements to include in the longitudinal files, you also must decide which cohorts to track and for how long. Because tracking numerous cohorts simultaneously is complex and usually shows little variation from one cohort to the next, it generally is sufficient to track every third fall entering class. Spring and summer entrants are tracked only if enrollments and characteristics of the students warrant separate tracking.

- *Include specific subgroup identifiers.* In addition to the obvious demographic variables, incorporate into the tracking file data elements to identify the student subgroups of interest to your institution. These may include identifiers for remedial students, minorities, nonnative English speakers, students participating in special programs, athletes, scholarship recipients, or other subgroups of special concern. While it is usually possible to go back to the original files to obtain additional data whose need was not foreseen, this can be time-consuming and costly. It is better to anticipate likely research questions and include the requisite data elements from the start.

* Conduct survey and focus group research. Survey and focus group research is valuable in illuminating key student decision points. Survey research is most useful when designed and implemented to add to the information yielded by the longitudinal file. Administer surveys to investigate student motivations, attitudes, and decision-making processes at key points during the college experience: at entry, after the first semester, and just prior to graduation. Focus groups add insights into student behavior beyond those obtained through mail surveys. Focus groups are a type of reality check. Through them, you may find student decision processes are more disorganized and uninformed than the responses elicited by multiple-choice questions. Focus groups can be used to assess institutional image and position, evaluate promotional materials, learn the special needs of particular student groups, and generate new ideas for improving or adding services.

* Zoom in and out to ensure relevancy. Enrollment management involves both a wide-angle view of the institution and a focused view of the student. To ensure that the data are relevant to the issues, you need to zoom in and out between the policy environment and information needs of decisionmakers and the details of student needs and progress. By identifying patterns of student behavior in the total enrollment, the institutional researcher provides meaningful analysis to executive managers who are more focused on FTEs and dollars.

ANALYSIS

Analytical techniques supporting enrollment management analysis range from simple to sophisticated. The analysis needed for the performance monitoring function is usually elementary. Calculations of yield ratios, percent change year-to-year, and retention

---

For information on student tracking systems, see:

Ewell, P.T., Parker, R., & Jones, D.P. (1988). *Establishing a longitudinal student tracking system: An implementation handbook.* National Center for Higher Education Management Systems, P.O. Drawer P, Boulder, CO 80301-9752.

Bers, T.H. (Ed.). (1989). Using student tracking systems effectively. *New Directions for Community Colleges, 66.* San Francisco: Jossey-Bass.

Palmer, J. (1990). *Accountability through student tracking: A review of the literature.* American Association of Community and Junior Colleges, National Center for Higher Education, One DuPont Circle, #410, Washington, DC 20036.

rates for student subgroups are simple but necessary and useful.

The biggest hurdle usually is in defining the base population or time period for analysis. The actual calculation of the indicators usually is easy. This is true even for estimating probabilities for simple cohort survival models. Crude survival rates can be calculated by answering the questions, "How many students of type A entering the college in term X were enrolled in term Y," or "How many students enrolled last term (who did not graduate) enrolled this term?" The resulting percentages then are arranged in

---

Attracting and retaining students is critical to maintaining the mission and health of your institution.

---

matrices displaying approximate student progression patterns.

Data from surveys and focus groups can be analyzed on their own or used as inputs in a more sophisticated model. The qualitative findings from focus group interviews are enlightening by themselves in identifying variables for subsequent, more quantitative analysis. For example, focus group research into college choice might identify net cost, distance from home, available social activities, and quality of student body as important factors. These qualitative findings could become quantifiable factors in an analysis of institutional competition utilizing college entrance test data.

Policy research analysis requires more sophisticated methods, such as multivariate analytical techniques. While a full discussion of these techniques is not possible in this chapter, some examples of applications to enrollment management follow.

Regression analysis. Multiple regression can predict freshman grade point averages from a linear combination of SAT scores, achievement test scores, high school GPA or percentile rank, and/or other variables. These predictions are useful in admissions decisions, selection of financial aid recipients, and estimates of subsequent retention. Stepwise logistic regression can predict student enrollment decisions or be used to investigate factors associated with academic dismissal or satisfactory performance after one term in college.

Factor analysis. Factor analysis can identify and define the underlying dimensions or factors contained in a larger set of variables. An application to enrollment management is identifying the underlying "product themes" in the confusing enrollment choices of continuing education students.

Cluster analysis. Cluster analysis can place cases into groups or clusters suggested by the data rather than by a priori definition. By balancing within-cluster homogeneity, between-cluster distance, and cluster size, the institutional researcher can derive a cluster set useful in number and differentiation. Examples of cluster analysis in enrollment management research include objectively classifying institutions in terms of size, selectivity, yield rates, SAT score means, student costs, and other quantitative data, determining prototypical student retention patterns, and identifying neighborhood lifestyle clusters in the surrounding service area for marketing purposes.

COMMUNICATION

Attracting and retaining students is critical to maintaining the mission and health of your institution. Recognition of the importance of this fact is leading more and more institutions to initiate enrollment management programs supported by student flow analysis. But even well-designed student flow analysis does not ensure success. Constant communication, supported by informative feedback loops and flexibility, is a critical component in an effective enrollment management program.

Adhering to several communication principles can facilitate enrollment management information sharing:

- *Know what data are needed.* The most fundamental principle is to provide decisionmakers with the data they need. To understand the data needs, it is critical that institutional researchers be part of the enrollment management team.

- *Know when the information is needed.* Institutional researchers can't influence a decision made yesterday. Both monitoring and policy research information

need to be available when required by decisionmakers.

- *Match format to analytical sophistication and learning preferences of recipients.* While you must use the analysis methods most appropriate to your research task, your presentation needs to be accessible to your audience. For example, a research paradigm to identify "top quality" applicants and build a related admissions rating procedure may use path, factor, and discriminant analyses. In sharing the results with an enrollment management team not versed in such techniques, focus on what was learned from the analysis rather than on methodology. If you lose people in long discussions about your methodology, the valuable insights discovered may be lost. Fortunately, many useful enrollment management analyses can be quite simple—especially those used for monitoring purposes.

- *Focus on one or two research questions at a time.* Although enrollment management is a comprehensive concept requiring extensive information, a series of brief reports, each focused on one or two policy issues, is more effective than a larger, all-inclusive analysis. For example, a report on student progression in a flow model may cover the entire spectrum of enrollment management, but in-depth investigations of individual student decision points are better shared in a series of reports.

Figure 5
Daily Fall Registration Status Report

As of August 22, 1990
With 9 Days Remaining in the Registration Period

	Fall 1989	Fall 1990	Percent Change
Total College			
Headcount	8,478	8,782	3.6%
Course Enrollments	22,966	22,997	0.1%
Credit Hours	70,912	71,566	0.9%
Average Credit Load	8.4	8.1	
Main Campus			
Course Enrollments	20,986	20,859	-0.6%
Credit Hours	64,642	64,880	0.4%
Extension Locations			
Course Enrollments	1,980	2,138	8.0%
Credit Hours	6,270	6,686	6.6%
Total Paid Hours	61,493	64,183	4.4%
Total Unpaid Hours	9,419	7,383	-21.6%

• *Use graphics selectively.* A few well-designed graphics can highlight important points and assist enrollment managers in understanding student trends. Too many, or poorly designed, graphics lose or mislead your audience. Integrate tables and graphics into your text or presentation. If you need to include detailed data, make your display as simple and clean as possible. **Figure 5** is a display of data needed by enrollment managers to monitor registration. The goal of this report is to provide managers with all the information they need at a glance.

REMEMBER

Efforts to influence the magnitude and composition of campus enrollments depend on timely and accurate information. Institutional research can provide performance monitoring indicators and policy research on all stages of student progress from inquiry and application, through enrollment and persistence, to successful completion and postgraduation follow-up.

However, many college and university enrollment management efforts fail because supplying data and analyses is only half the battle. Effective enrollment management efforts depend on

23

institutional commitment, good and timely analysis, careful coordination, and constant communication feedback.

With all of these requirements, many may ask why bother with enrollment management. The question is legitimate and should be carefully considered in terms of the institution's mission, leadership, and environment.

While institutional researchers alone cannot ensure the success of the enrollment management program, they play a crucial role at all phases of the process. You can do this best by understanding fully the policy/decision context and by designing analyses and monitoring processes that respond directly to your institution's changing needs.

Student Impacts

Jean Endo

ISSUES

Longitudinal student impact studies examine the effects of intervention strategies on student outcomes related to learning, personal and social growth, academic ability, and career development. Intervention strategies may include academic initiatives, such as innovative curricula or residential academic programs; student support efforts, such as academic skills development classes or retention programs for high-risk students; or cultural and social activities, such as those for minority group students. Measures of student outcomes may include test scores, grades, written reports, portfolios, and/or self-assessments on questionnaires. Impact studies often are conducted for one-, two-, or four-year periods following college entrance. Their characteristics can vary depending upon the mission and circumstances of the institution.

This chapter outlines some basic principles for conducting a longitudinal impact study associated with undergraduate student development. This type of study might be undertaken to show the types of intervention strategies that are important for enhancing student development, to determine the magnitude and significance of such development, and to identify specific interventions that might be more effective for particular types of students.

BACKGROUND

If you are unfamiliar with research literature on student impacts, start by reviewing useful general works, such as Astin (1991) and Pascarella and Terenzini (1991). Take a look, also, at older, "classic" work, including Feldman and Newcomb (1969) and Pace (1979).

Jean Endo is the assistant director of the Office of Institutional Research at the University of Colorado at Boulder. She currently is editor of AIR Forum Publications and a consulting editor of Research in Higher Education.

For the most recent overviews of student development impact studies, see:

Astin, A.W. (1991). *Assessment for excellence: The philosophy and practice of assessment and evaluation in higher education.* New York: American Council on Education, Macmillan.

Pascarella, E.T., & Terenzini, P.T. (1991). *How college affects students.* San Francisco: Jossey-Bass.

The "classics" on student development and impact studies include:

Feldman, K.A., & Newcomb, T.M. (1969). *The impact of college on students: Vol. I. An analysis of four decades of research.* San Francisco: Jossey-Bass.

Pace, C.R. (1979). *Measuring outcomes of college.* San Francisco: Jossey-Bass.

DATA

Initial Steps

Before you begin designing your longitudinal impact study, you will most likely face one of two possibilities. The first is that you need to conduct a study examining the effects of a wide range of loosely defined or unspecified intervention strategies on a wide range of loosely defined or unspecified student outcomes. We will call this **Situation A**. You might find yourself in Situation A, for instance, when your institution plans to conduct a comprehensive assessment of outcomes. The second possibility, **Situation B**, is that you know at the outset that you need to do a more focused study on a specific intervention strategy (or strategies) and set of outcomes.

Situation A. If you find yourself facing Situation A, you first need to identify the student outcomes and related intervention strategies you want to examine. Proceed through the steps outlined in **Figure 1**.

Based on the material you have gathered to this point, select a set of student outcomes for your study

---

Figure 1

Identifying Outcomes and Interventions

Step 1 *Review published taxonomies of student outcomes.*

- See, for example, Astin's (1991) taxonomy classifying outcomes by three dimensions: type, data, and time.

- Become aware of a wide range of possible outcomes.

- Examine both affective and cognitive types of outcomes because cognitive development is often related to affective development. Pascarella & Terenzini (1991) describe such outcomes as follows: "Cognitive outcomes have to do with the utilization of higher-order intellectual processes, such as knowledge acquisiton, decision-making, synthesis, and reasoning. Affective outcomes are attitudes, values, self-concepts, aspirations, and personality dispositions" (p.5).

Step 2 *Interview top administrators.*

- Identify high priority student outcomes and related intervention strategies (e.g., new, existing, and planned).

- Determine areas where your study can best contribute to short- and long-term planning.

- Determine the types of intervention strategies top administrators are most willing to support.

Step 3 *Interview other individuals involved with programs who are knowledgeable about the student outcomes identified by top administrators.*

- Ask interviewees to identify what they see as effective intervention strategies.

- Ask interviewees to identify differences they observe in outcomes for specific student subgroups, for instance, racial/ethnic, gender, age, or economic subgroups.

Step 4 *Gather existing internal reports, studies, and minutes of administrative and governing board meetings.*

- Identify issues related to student outcomes and information on student characteristics.

- Identify additional outcomes to be studied.

along with corresponding intervention strategies. To link outcomes and intervention strategies, it is helpful to think of research questions. A research question identifies a specific relationship between an outcome (or set of outcomes) and an intervention strategy (or set of strategies). Frame your research questions so that the answers can be easily translated into policy recommendations. An example of a research question is: Do skills taught by a new English workshop series to students during the freshman year improve students' writing abilities?

Situation B. You are now at the point where you would be if you had been originally faced with Situation B instead of Situation A. We will continue the discussion using the following illustrative Situation B example:

Assume that an assessment committee asks you to research the effect on student outcomes of participation by freshmen for one year in a mentoring program designed to increase student-faculty interaction. The outcomes of interest include educational aspirations, confidence with interpersonal skills, and development of critical thinking skills. Special attention needs to be given to differences by racial/ethnic group and gender.

The first step is to interview people who designed and/or administered the intervention strategy in your study. This will allow you to identify important variables. Talk also to a sample of faculty and student participants.

Then, to get additional ideas, review the relevant research literature. Focus on the student outcomes and intervention strategy in your study. Remember to look for possible differences in outcomes for specific student subgroups. When considering differences by race/ethnicity, do not assume that Asian Americans, Hispanics/Latinos, and Native Americans/American Indians are monolithic groups whose members have the same backgrounds, experiences, expectations, and abilities. For the student-faculty interaction study, a review of the literature will reveal, for instance, that it is important to distinguish between formal and informal

> Two classic models on student integration are:
>
> Spady, W.G. (1971). Dropouts from higher education: Toward an empirical model. *Interchange*, 2, 38-62.
> Tinto, V. (1987). *Leaving college: Rethinking the causes and cures of student attrition.* Chicago: University of Chicago Press.

student-faculty interaction. Further, the literature may indicate that some Asian Americans who are not fluent in the English language (e.g., newly immigrated Vietnamese, Laotian, and Cambodian students) might, as a result, be reluctant to interact with faculty.

As you review the literature, you may run across conceptual frameworks or models that help explain particular student outcomes. Such models identify key variables and suggest relationships between intervention strategies and outcomes. For example, Spady's (1971) and Tinto's (1987) models show how persistence is related to the degree to which a student is integrated into an institution's academic and social systems. The literature demonstrating and extending these models is extensive.

One recommended method of organizing your variables is to think in terms of Astin's "input-environment-output" model (Astin, 1991, pp. 16-37). **Input** includes the outcomes variables measured at an initial point in time prior to the intervention strategy. Input may also include background factors students bring with them to college that can influence the outcomes variables unless such factors are controlled, for example, demographic characteristics, academic ability, expectations for college, goals for attending college, and values. These factors are important because previous research indicates that they can have a major impact on outcomes. **Environment** includes the intervention strategy variables. Envi-ronment may also include variables related to other factors that can affect the outcomes under consideration, such as other educational programs. **Output** includes the outcomes variables that are measured at some point after the corresponding intervention strategy has occurred. For the student-faculty interaction study, the relevant variables might be organized as seen in **Figure 2.**

The Study Sample

You are now at the stage where you must plan the collection of data for your longitudinal impact

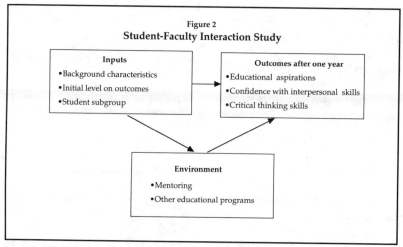

Figure 2
Student-Faculty Interaction Study

study. Most impact studies focus on a specific cohort (or cohorts) of students. Often, as in the case of the student-faculty interaction study, it is best to define the cohort as consisting of all newly enrolled freshmen with no previous college experience from a specific fall term.

Generally, the number of students you will need in your study sample depends upon the homogeneity of your cohort in terms of background characteristics, the number of analyses you plan to do on specific student subgroups, and the number of years you intend to study these students. For a four-year impact study, it may be necessary to include all or a large number of students in a cohort because many will probably no longer be enrolled after four years. For a one-year study, it usually is acceptable to select a smaller random sample of students because a high percentage will still be enrolled at the end of one year. However, in the case of the student-faculty interaction study, it might be best to include all incoming freshmen to ensure adequate numbers of students from the various racial/ethnic subgroups.

Longitudinal Data Files

The two most important sources of data for your longitudinal impact study are institutional data files and questionnaires. Your institution's computer data files probably include such admissions-related information as students'

> **For details on sampling, see:**
> Sudman, S. (1976). *Applied sampling.* New York: Academic Press.
> Kalton, G. (1983). *Introduction to survey sampling.* Beverly Hills, CA: Sage.

demographic characteristics, college entrance test scores, and high school grades. These data files also will include course-related information for each enrolled student. For the student-faculty interaction study, data files can provide information on students' back-

ground characteristics as well as academic progress.

A useful method of organizing the collection of data from institutional data files is to identify when your institution gathers and records information on the variables needed for your study. For example, in early summer, your institution may collect information on such variables as gender, race/ethnicity, citizenship, college entrance scores, and intended major. At the end of each term, it will collect data for all enrolled students on such variables as cumulative college grade point average, credits earned, major, and dropout status.

However, institutional data files are developed for the operational use of offices on your campus and not for research purposes. As a result, they may lack data critical for your study. To fully understand the data, you should talk with several users of these files. If you need additional data, plan to collect your own by using questionnaires. For example, your institution's data files may only identify students' race/ethnicity in general categories such as "Hispanic" and "Asian." If you need more specificity, a detailed question about race/ethnicity will have to be included on a questionnaire.

Questionnaires

After you have identified the data that can be obtained from institutional data files, you will need to construct questionnaires to gather other important data. A minimum of two types of questionnaires are necessary for a one-year impact study: an entering freshman questionnaire and an educational experience survey administered after the cohort has been at your institution for one year. For a four-year impact study, a graduating student survey also is needed and should be administered after the cohort has been at your institution for four years.

Plan to send the freshman questionnaire to students in the late summer prior to fall registration. Alternatively, it might be administered during a pre-semester orientation session. This questionnaire should include questions on background characteristics not contained in institutional data files, such as family income, and questions that measure the initial values of your outcomes variables. Plan to send the educational experience questionnaire near the end of the academic year. This questionnaire should include questions on outcomes variables and intervention strategies. For a four-year impact study, plan to send the graduating student questionnaire to students who are still enrolled at the end of the fourth academic year. This questionnaire should include questions similar to those on the educational experience questionnaire as well as questions about future educational and career plans.

You may develop questionnaires yourself or with the help of a committee. Keep your input-environment-output model and research questions in mind as you map out the variables that will be included on specific instruments. There will be no need to collect information already available from your institution's data files unless you want to build in some redundancy on a few key variables to help you assess the reliability of your data. With adequate time, you will be able to develop your own instruments tailored to the unique characteristics of your students and institution. You might also consider purchasing

Longitudinal impact studies are essential to any examination of the effects of educational intervention strategies.

commercially available instruments. For some examples, see Ewell (1985).

You should construct the educational experience questionnaire before the freshman questionnaire. As you develop the educational experience questionnaire, you will discover items that also need to be included on the freshman questionnaire. For example, it is important to include on the freshman questionnaire each outcomes variable that appears on the educational experience survey. The single best predictor of any student outcome after one year is the value of the same outcome at the start of college. The wording of outcomes measures should be identical on both questionnaires.

There are some technical issues you will need to consider in constructing questionnaires. In measuring specific variables, it is necessary to be aware of so-called "ceiling and cellar effects." If some students are expected to measure very high (or very low) on an outcomes variable on one questionnaire, the variable response categories, or scale, should be designed so that there is room to measure "improvement" (or decline) on this outcomes variable on a subsequent questionnaire. It also is important to be aware of regression effects. A student who initially measures very high on an outcomes variable (or a student sample selected on the basis of high initial values on an outcomes variable) will tend to measure lower on that outcomes variable (i.e., regress to the mean of the entire student population) on a subsequent questionnaire. Likewise, a student (or sample of students) who initially measures very low on an outcomes variable will tend to measure higher on that outcomes variable on a subsequent questionnaire.

In constructing questionnaires, you should follow basic principles. A good reference is Dillman (1978). It also is necessary to take into account what is already known about the institution and its students. For instance, income response categories should reflect the known range of students' family incomes, and financial questions should allow for the higher tuition paid by out-of-state students. Give special attention to

arranging questions in a logical and meaningful fashion. Determine the physical layout of your questionnaires according to its convenience for respondents, not by data entry or cost considerations. For example, although mark-sense forms can reduce the cost of data entry, these may be cumbersome and difficult for students to complete.

An important administrator, such as the institution's president, should write a cover letter seeking students' participation in your study. The letter should include a statement of the purpose of the study, describe how the results will be used, and provide assurances of confidentiality.

You should have relevant institutional administrators and staff review a preliminary draft of each questionnaire and its accompanying cover letter and then pretest them on a sample of students. Allow ample time for your pretest. One purpose of the pretest is to identify ambiguous and sensitive questions. Another is to determine whether a particular questionnaire is too long and whether the questions are written in an appropriate manner. A final purpose is to make sure respondents feel each questionnaire is important and that the results will be used to improve their education. Revise your instruments to reflect comments you receive from the pretest.

After the final drafts of the questionnaires are completed, you might consider photomechanically reducing their size. For example, the front title page, the cover letter, and six questionnaire pages will fit on four 3 1/2-inch columns of legal-sized paper. The resulting questionnaire is lightweight, inexpensive to mail, and compact for future storage.

Before distributing the questionnaires, you will need to give each a unique five-digit number corresponding to a specific student. Students generally prefer to see a five-digit number rather than their Social Security numbers on questionnaires. However, the cover letter should explain the reason for this number and provide assurances that responses will be kept confidential.

Plan to send individual questionnaires through the mail along with self-addressed and stamped return envelopes to make it easy for students to respond. You might think about ways to reduce mailing costs. For instance, it may be possible to include the freshman questionnaire with registration materials sent to new freshmen. You also could mail the educational experience survey through your campus mail system to students living on campus.

It will be necessary to get a high percentage of responses so that you have enough cases to conduct your analyses and to eliminate sample biases. Consider sending a postcard reminder to all of the students about a week after questionnaires are mailed, and send another follow-up questionnaire to nonrespondents about two weeks after mailing the postcard reminder. In addition, consider

following up later with telephone calls, especially to members of student subgroups that are especially important to your study. For maximum response rates, do not plan to mail the questionnaire around examination periods or school vacations.

Building the Data Set

Once you have planned the collection of data for your longitudinal impact study, you should think about the construction of a data set. To create a data set, you first must download the necessary information from your institution's data files to your personal computer or to another computer using the appropriate software. For assistance, you will want to consult with a systems analyst at your campus who is familiar with the institution's data files. Then, you need to code the responses from each questionnaire and enter them into your newly created data set. You may wish to develop special codes for responses to open-ended questions (see Warwick & Lininger, 1975, pp. 239-248, 253-254).

The following example using the student-faculty interaction study illustrates the process of constructing a one-year data set. First, download relevant background and other pre-college data for the students in the cohort from institutional data files at the beginning of the fall term to create the data set. Next, add data from the freshman questionnaire to the data set. Third, at the end of each term, add enrollment data perti-

For more information on the design of your study, see:

Warwick, D.P., & Lininger, C.A. (1975). *The sample survey: Theory and practice.* New York: McGraw-Hill.

Dillman, D.A. (1978). *Mail and telephone surveys.* New York: Wiley.

Karweit, N.L., & Meyers, E. (1983). Computers in survey research. In P.H. Rossi, J.D. Wright, & A.B. Anderson (Eds.), *Handbook of survey research.* (pp. 379-414). Orlando: Academic Press.

Ewell, P.T. (1985). Appendix. In P.T. Ewell (Ed.), Assessing educational outcomes. *New Directions for Institutional Research, 47,* 121-122. San Francisco: Jossey Bass.

nent to your study. The final step is to add data from the educational experience survey. For studies longer than one year, the data file is updated with subsequent enrollment and questionnaire data.

Each addition to the data set should match student identification numbers from institutional data files and the questionnaire identification numbers given to each student. These matching procedures make it possible to link data on the same student from several different sources. Without this matching, it is impossible to examine variables from two or more different sources in the same bivariate or multivariate analyses, and the investigation of changes on specific variables is precluded.

After each addition is made to the data set, you must check for possible coding, data entry, or response errors. For a discussion on such errors and data-cleaning procedures, see Karweit and Meyers (1983, pp. 392-397).

ANALYSIS

Once you have actually collected the data for your longitudinal impact study and constructed a data set, the systematic analysis of data is critical to the success of your project. Earlier, in the design of your study, you specified the variable relationships you wished to examine. These now will provide the structure and direction for your data analysis. Begin your actual analysis by examining the characteristics of the student respondents. Determine whether or not these students are representative of those in the entire cohort in terms of major input, environmental, and output variables. You will need to make adjustments if the student respondents are not representative of the entire cohort (see Hurtado, Astin, Korn, & Dey, 1987).

When analyzing your data, simple descriptive procedures, like cross-tabulations and bivariate measures of association, are useful. However, multivariate statistical techniques are particularly appropriate for investigating the impact of intervention strategies on student outcomes. It is impossible to even begin a discussion of statistical techniques within the space available here. Instead, a few suggestions and references will be presented.

If you have only a minimal understanding of statistics, obtain the assistance of staff or faculty at your institution who have the necessary expertise. Involve these individuals in your study from

33

the very beginning. Their input during the design of your study and the data collection will prevent many problems from occurring during the analysis phase.

If you have an understanding of statistical techniques up through least squares multiple regression, review the methodological appendices in Terenzini and Pascarella (1991a) and Astin (1991). Pay particular attention to discussions of causal modeling, a method that focuses on the direct and indirect causal influences within a theoretically guided system of variables. This method is especially relevant if you have organized your variables in terms of Astin's input-environment-output model.

Typically, causal modeling makes use of ordinary least squares multiple regression or LISREL (linear structural relations) techniques. Moline's (1988) article provides additional references that can be consulted if you wish to master these techniques.

In reading this statistical literature it is important to understand the advantages and disadvantages of various techniques and the assumptions that must be met. Pay particular attention to instructions for interpreting findings. Many researchers make the mistake of using statistical techniques without understanding how to distinguish between important and unimportant results. Remember to estimate the magnitude of changes over time in outcomes that are impacted by an intervention strategy (i.e., effect sizes). For more

discussion, see Terenzini and Pascarella (1991, pp. 86-87).

Once you have completed your data analyses, you need to interpret your findings and develop recommendations. Interpret the findings in a broad manner that has practical implications for your institution. Take care to distinguish

> **For more information on data analysis, see:**
> Hurtado, S., Astin, A., Korn, W., & Dey, E. (1987). *The American college student.* Higher Education Research Institute, Graduate School of Education, University of California at Los Angeles, Los Angeles, CA 90024. Phone: 213/825-1925.
> Moline, A.E. (1988). Causal modeling for institutional researchers. In B.D. Yancey (Ed.), Applying statistics in institutional research. *New Directions for Institutional Research, 58,* 61-76. San Francisco: Jossey-Bass.
> Terenzini, P.T., & Pascarella, E.T. (1991). Twenty years of research on college students: Lessons for future research. *Research in Higher Education, 32*(1), 83-92.

strong from weak findings. Where possible, make recommendations from specific sets of findings. Consider the cost-effectiveness of alternative recommendations. Have your institution's administrators and other staff who are familiar with the topics under investigation review preliminary versions of your study's findings, interpretations, and recommendations.

COMMUNICATION

The findings from your impact study can be presented in a report that includes (1) a one- to two-page executive summary, (2) a statement of the study objectives and reasons why the research is important to the institution, (3) a description of any conceptual frameworks and/or models used, (4) a discussion of the study design and sampling method, (5) a description of the characteristics of the sample compared with the total number of students in the cohort, (6) a discussion of the data analyses (7) a summary of the findings, (8) a conclusion, (9) recommendations, and (10) appendices (e.g., copies of the questionnaires and cover letters).

Begin the report with a one- or two-page executive summary that describes major findings and recommendations. This summary allows busy individuals to review your study quickly and to decide whether and when to read the entire report.

Describe the data analyses in a logical fashion, for example, in a developmental or chronological order. If numerous analyses were undertaken, describe the major analyses in detail and summarize others. Present analyses for the entire cohort before those for student subgroups, unless certain subgroups are the primary objects of attention.

Describe complex statistical analyses in a straightforward and simple manner. Where appropriate, supplement these with bivariate tables. For instance, after explaining in a multiple regression analysis that variable A had a certain effect on variable B, include a bivariate table with percentages.

Make sure all of your tables are easy to read.

Present recommendations at the end of a report. Put these in a logical order, for example, those that are the most cost-effective before those that are the least cost-effective, those that have the broadest impacts before those that have lesser impacts, or those based on the strongest findings before those based on weaker findings. Since recommendations often receive more attention than the rest of a report, write them with great care.

Have relevant institutional administrators and staff review a preliminary version of your report. Distribute the final version of your report to university administrators and staff who can implement the recommendations.

For a few offices or academic units, consider producing customized reports. Each of these will focus on a particular issue important to the office or unit. Keep these reports brief. Limit the narrative to a few pages and supplement with data tables or graphs.

For further suggestions on communicating the findings of your study, see: Ewell, P.T. (Ed.). (1989). Enhancing information use in decision-making. *New Directions for Institutional Research, 64.* San Francisco: Jossey-Bass.

REMEMBER

Good impact studies must be well designed. Take the time to thoroughly interview relevant individuals, review the appropriate research literature, and specify relationships between key variables. Be sensitive to differences between student subgroups and keep in mind the possible implications of your study for policy and program improvement.

Collect your data in a careful manner. Make sure your sample is representative of the student population to which you want to generalize your results. Also, make sure that any questionnaires you construct measure all of the necessary variables and that they are put together following sound principles.

Do a systematic analysis of your data using appropriate statistical techniques. Do not be reluctant to seek outside assistance for this (or any other) task. Interpret your findings in a manner that has practical implications for your institution.

Finally, remember that impact studies usually require a good deal of time, effort, and other resources. Always be prepared to commit enough of these scarce commodities so that you can successfully execute and complete your study.

Faculty Demand

Michael D. McGuire

ISSUES

Even casual readers of lay and professional publications over the past few years have been struck by the attention devoted to possible faculty shortages in this decade. The prospects of dwindling and demoralized faculties, larger classes taught by overburdened and underqualified instructors, and cut-throat competition for top candidates from graduate programs have led to considerable alarm and increasing amounts of research at the institutional and national levels.

As an institutional researcher in this climate, you will be asked to provide valid and reliable information on the following set of critical issues:

- Will there be a **national** faculty shortage? How bad will it be? When will it strike? Which institutions and academic disciplines will be most affected?

- What will be the **local** impact of these shortages if they do indeed materialize?

- How many faculty will your institution need to hire in each year of the next 20 years?

Michael D. McGuire is the director of Planning and Institutional Research at Franklin and Marshall College, Lancaster, Pennsylvania. He is a member of AIR's Data Advisory Committee.

- What initiatives can be undertaken to prevent a faculty shortage and a decline in the quality of your educational programs?

Although there may be striking differences between local and national concerns in this area, you should develop a working knowledge of national trends for several reasons. First, it is strategically important to know the level of competition for available faculty at any point in time. Even if your institution needs to hire only one or two faculty members in a given department in a given year, there will be times when that modest task will be much harder to accomplish due to demand peaks nationally. Under extremely competitive circumstances you may choose either to hire early or to defer hiring until the supply and demand differential is more favorable.

Second, even if you plan to hire only a small number of faculty during a discipline's low-demand years, it is important to know the market conditions immediately before and after your hiring period. The available supply of faculty may be less than projected if significant numbers of competitor institutions hire early (i.e., A.B.D.) during a preceding high-demand period. Similarly, competition may be more intense than expected if other institutions are stockpiling faculty in anticipation of a subsequent high-demand cycle.

The purpose of this chapter is to acquaint you with some of the methodologies and information resources that can help you develop and monitor local projections within the larger context of the evolving national professoriate. The emphasis of this chapter is on describing the tools for acquiring and analyzing data rather than on summaries and interpretations of previous studies.

The literature on faculty supply and demand will continue to grow, and later studies will almost certainly contradict many of the early projections. Of greater practical usefulness to you as an institutional researcher is the ability to establish supply and demand baselines at your institution, to identify potential problems in and solutions for faculty hiring as early as possible, and to track your institution's progress in recruiting and retaining needed faculty.

BACKGROUND

Depending upon how broadly you define "faculty supply and demand," the current literature base is either unmanageably extensive or woefully sparse. The reason for this ambiguity lies in the difficulty in disentangling supply and demand analyses from a host of other faculty and labor market issues. The latter include faculty (and nonfaculty) compensation and working conditions, student enrollment projections and the many variables that determine them, economic and political factors at both the institutional and societal levels, the evolving missions of higher education in this country and others, the health and productivity of graduate programs, and the attitudes and aspirations and cumulative life experiences of contemporary undergraduates. A considerable body of research touches on one or more

The academic disciplines will experience supply and demand imbalances at different times.

of these issues; a much more limited body directly addresses the construction and validation of faculty demand models.

In general, most of the studies projecting faculty demand over the next 10 to 20 years converge on the following conclusions:

- Demand for new faculty hires at the institutional and national levels will increase substantially in the late 1990s and beyond.

- Supply of traditional postdoctoral faculty will fail to keep pace with demand.

- Some academic disciplines will experience a more severe supply and demand imbalance than others, and different academic disciplines will experience supply and demand imbalances at different times.

Perhaps the most comprehensive review of the faculty supply and demand literature can be found in two publications by the Western Interstate Commission for Higher Education (WICHE) (1991, 1992). Each document presents a summary and critical analysis of the major studies of faculty supply and demand and other related issues.

For reviews of faculty demand literature, see:

Western Interstate Commission for Higher Education. (1991). *The literature on factors affecting faculty supply and demand: An annotated bibliography*.

Western Interstate Commission for Higher Education. (1992). *Bringing into focus the factors affecting faculty supply and demand: A primer for higher education and state policymakers*.

WICHE Publications, P.O. Drawer P, Boulder, CO 80301-9752. Phone: 303/541-0290.

Three recent investigations using national samples are Bowen and Sosa (1989), McGuire and Price (1990), and Lozier and Dooris (1991). Each study addresses faculty retirement, nonretirement attrition, and total faculty size and hiring needs over the next 20 years.

The studies differ somewhat in the nature of their data, the institutions sampled, and their specific conclusions. Each study has its unique strengths. For example, the Bowen and Sosa study specializes in its detailed presentation of an enrollment-driven faculty projection model. The Lozier and Dooris study examines factors influencing faculty retirement decisions, particularly pension programs. The McGuire and Price study explores preliminary data

Faculty demand studies using national samples include:

Bowen, W.G., & Sosa, J.A. (1989). *Prospects for faculty in the arts and sciences: A study of factors affecting demand and supply, 1987-2012*. Princeton, NJ: Princeton University Press.

McGuire, M.D., & Price, J.A. (1990). *Previewing the professoriate of the 21st century: A multi-institutional analysis of faculty supply and demand*. Paper presented at the 25th annual meeting of the Society for College and University Planning, Atlanta, GA.

Lozier, G.G., & Dooris, M.J. (1991). *Faculty retirement projections beyond 1994: Effects of policy on individual choice*. Boulder, CO: Western Interstate Commission on Higher Education.

on recent hiring practices and on sources of new faculty.

Other recent studies of national significance are the American Council on Education's (ACE) *Campus Trends* surveys (El-Khawas, 1990, 1991) and the Project on Faculty Retirement (Rees & Smith, 1991). The 1990 and 1991 ACE surveys revealed difficulties in hiring sufficient numbers of high-quality faculty at many higher education institutions, well before the period of severe imbalance projected in the three studies cited above. Given current levels of hiring stress, some increases in these stressors since the 1989 ACE survey (El-Khawas, 1989), and the probability that higher enrollments and more faculty retirements are almost certainly up the road, the alarm generated by these reports appears warranted. It is also noteworthy, however, that as a result of fiscal constraints and program realignments, some institutions reported a decrease in

El-Khawas, E. (1989). *Campus trends, 1989.*

El-Khawas, E. (1990). *Campus trends, 1990.*

El-Khawas, E. (1991). *Campus trends, 1991.*

American Council on Education, One Dupont Circle, Washington, DC 20036-1193. Phone: 202/939-9450.

Rees, A., & Smith, S.P. (1991). *Faculty retirement in the arts and sciences.* Princeton, NJ: Princeton University Press.

faculty hiring stressors and expected shortages between the 1990 and 1991 surveys.

The Project on Faculty Retirement (Rees & Smith, 1991) found that the end of mandatory faculty retirement policies in the 1990s will probably have little or no impact on the timing of faculty retirements. This result has clear implications for projecting faculty needs. Among other things, it suggests that the retention of faculty who would have been forced to retire before 1994 may not be a significant factor in overcoming the supply and demand imbalances in the last half of this decade. It remains to be seen whether delayed- or partial-retirement incentive programs will be effective counterforces to a potentially massive increase in faculty hiring needs.

The reader is encouraged to review these studies. The WICHE reports provide an excellent overview and a thorough, up-to-date list of references on faculty supply and demand. In any event, the national literature is a necessary but not sufficient component of your institution's study of faculty flow. Local data will be needed to identify the specific challenges that you will face in the years ahead.

DATA

While a review of the national literature can provide a context for your institutional studies and some ideas for local research, the most important questions that you will need to address involve the collection, analysis, and reporting of data at your institution. There are several key methodological considerations to consider in carrying out this research agenda.

Briefly, demand for faculty can be viewed as a function of two factors: **replacement need** and **growth**. A number of market and

Demand for faculty can be viewed as a function of replacement need and growth.

institutional conditions will influence each of these: for replacement need, the rate of and reasons for departure from an institution's faculty, and perhaps the profession, and experiential differences among current faculty (e.g., age at hire, rank at hire, age at retirement, years in pension plan, promotional patterns); for growth, institutional enrollment trends and financial stability (e.g., tuition and non-tuition revenue growth and competing expenditure pressures). In order to arrive at accurate quantitative projections of faculty supply and demand, it is important to have an understanding of your own institution's faculty flow trends.

Historical Data

As a first step it is useful to examine faculty hiring experiences at your institution over the last 10 years, with special attention to the past two to three years. A sample database, compiled by faculty rank and academic department, is presented in **Table 1**. Because of space limitations, this example includes only faculty at the full and associate professor ranks and examines only a handful of departments in the natural sciences. The assistant professor and instructor ranks and all academic disciplines would be included in an actual model. Furthermore, the tabulation of a single year's data in this example would be repeated for each of the past 3 to 10 years to permit the tracking of change over time.

Some faculty flow models are aggregated by faculty age cohort rather than academic rank. While age and rank are positively correlated, it seems logical to aggregate by rank for two reasons. First, the correlation between age and rank may be diminishing as time to doctorate and age at doctoral initiation increase, producing greater age variations in the entry-level professoriate (this correlation was 0.64 for the fall 1989 faculty cohort in McGuire and Price, 1990). Second, the decisions and circumstances that determine faculty flow are often linked to rank transitions (e.g., promotion or failure to achieve promotion at one's institution, movement with promotion to another institution),

and retention rates vary considerably by rank. The small handful of institutions without faculty ranks, however, can substitute age cohort for rank in developing a flow model.

The historical model also features subtotals for academic divisions or domains. These can be useful summary measures for deans who are responsible for entire divisions. They also highlight departmental overlap or interdisciplinary possibilities (e.g., biochemistry) that can provide some hiring flexibility, an important consideration for reasons of program development or hiring efficiency.

In addition to the data elements in **Table 1**, four other types of information should be compiled historically:

- *age of faculty at retirement,*
- *reasons for nonretirement exit or movement across ranks* (e.g., promotion within the institution, movement to another institution or to a nonfaculty line of work, failure to attain tenure or contract renewal, death or disability),
- *source of hire* (e.g., recent Ph.D., A.B.D., faculty or administrative employment at another institution, administrative or part-time faculty employment at your institution, nonacademic employment), and
- *institutional ranking of new hires* (i.e., the institution's first vs. second vs. third choice among finalists in the applicant pool).

Table 1							
Faculty Flow Data							
Sample Year							
		Full-time				Part-time	
Full Professors							
Department	Total	New Hires	Promoted In	Retirees	Other Exits	Total	New
Astronomy	10	0	1	1	1	0	0
Biology	19	1	2	2	1	0	0
Chemistry	16	1	2	1	1	0	0
Geology	11	0	0	1	0	0	0
Physics	12	1	1	0	1	0	0
All Natural Sciences	68	3	6	5	4	0	0
Associate Professors							
Astronomy	11	1	1	0	1	0	0
Biology	16	2	2	0	3	1	1
Chemistry	14	2	2	1	3	1	1
Geology	11	1	1	0	1	0	0
Physics	12	1	1	0	2	0	0
All Natural Sciences	64	7	7	1	10	2	2

NOTE: These figures were not derived from actual institutional data.

All faculty ranks and disciplines and a 3- to 10-year time span would be used in actual modeling.

Contemporary Data

The historical data will describe the context within which your present faculty has evolved. This context provides assumptions for projecting future faculty needs, although the baseline for those projections is your current faculty. You will require a more detailed dataset on the current faculty, preferably at the individual faculty member rather than department level.

Table 2 presents a list of data elements you need to include in this faculty data set. All full-time faculty presently at your institution should be included. Part-time faculty are typically hired from different sources, under different conditions, and for different lengths of time, thus rendering most temporal and experiential parameters irrelevant. Since the focus of supply and demand analysis is on full-time faculty, we will concentrate most of our discussion on that group (although a parallel file can certainly be established for institutions wishing to track part-time faculty with precision).

Table 2	
Contemporary Faculty Flow Data	
Track status (tenure, visiting)	Years since appointment
Department	Rank at hire
Date of birth	Gender
Age	Ethnicity
Rank	Previous employment status or position
Years in rank	Previous employment site
Years since terminal degree	Expected retirement year

The model does not distinguish between tenure track and nontenure track faculty in estimating hiring needs, as it assumes that all full-time faculty perform valuable services and that all departures will be replaced unless otherwise noted through a negative growth rate. It nevertheless may be useful to collect data on track status because of the trade-off between the greater institutional flexibility afforded by nontenure track positions versus the greater attractiveness of tenure track positions to top candidates in a competitive hiring environment.

ANALYSIS

The historical data will contribute five types of information for describing the characteristics of, and projecting the demand for, your institution's future faculty (see **Table 3**).

Attrition, or the rate of faculty exits from your institution, is a primary consideration. There are two annual percentages of interest in the sample model: percent of faculty retiring and percent of faculty leaving your institution for other reasons. A more precise model would include separate percentages for the different exit reasons listed above. Of special interest are (a) the distinction between voluntary exits (e.g., received a better offer from another institution or profession) and involuntary exits (e.g., denied tenure) and (b) potential strategies for reducing these attrition rates. Note that past retirement rates are not used to project future retirement rates; your current faculty's age distribution and your historical retirement age trends will be used for this projection.

Promotion represents change in status (rank) within the institution rather than net loss from the institutional or national faculty. It is nonetheless important to track because it may reflect, at least indirectly, the potential for future attrition (since different ranks experience different exit rates for

43

different reasons). Promotion rates can be influenced by institutional policies (i.e., timing of promotion reviews) and professional standards. These vary across institutions and across time within the same institution.

Similarly, **rank proportions** represent the balance among senior, intermediate, and junior faculty at your institution. A "top-heavy" institution will usually have different resource and faculty attrition distributions than a "bottom-heavy" institution. Specifically, a disproportionate num-ber of full professors may portend higher retirement but lower nonretirement attrition, as well as the need to devote more resources for faculty compensation; a disproportionate number of assistant professors, on the other hand, may portend higher turnover and perhaps greater competition for tenure.

Growth rates (for all ranks combined) describe the overall growth pattern—positive or negative—of your institution's faculty in the recent past. As was the case for retirements, past growth patterns

Table 3

Faculty Flow Measures

(Percentages)

	Astro-nomy	Biology	Chemistry	Geology	Physics	All Natural Sciences
Full Professors						
% of All Full-time Faculty	50.0	55.1	52.5	52.3	48.9	52.1
% Retiring Annually	9.5	7.9	9.8	4.5	4.5	7.4
% Other Institutional Exits Annually	5.0	2.6	3.1	4.2	8.7	4.4
% Newly Promoted	9.5	7.9	9.6	0.0	4.2	6.6
Associate Professors						
% of All Full-time Faculty	50.0	44.9	47.5	47.7	51.1	47.9
% Retiring Annually	0.0	0.0	3.6	0.0	4.2	1.6
% Other Institutional Exits Annually	5.0	8.1	8.3	9.5	8.3	7.8
% Newly Promoted	9.5	9.6	14.3	9.5	8.3	10.4
All Ranks						
Part-time as % of All Faculty	0.0	5.8	5.1	0.0	0.0	2.7
New Part-time as % of All Part-time	0.0	25.0	75.0	0.0	0.0	58.3
% Retiring Annually	4.8	4.3	6.8	2.3	4.3	4.6
% Other Institutional Exits Annually	4.8	4.3	5.1	6.8	8.5	5.7
% Newly Promoted	9.5	8.7	11.9	4.5	6.4	8.4
Annual Growth Rate (Full-time)	0.0	2.9	3.4	0.0	4.3	2.3

Note: Institutions that use rank with part-time faculty could also apply the full-time measures to their part-time faculty.

The ranks of instructor and assistant professor and the ranks of all academic departments would be included in actual modeling.

cannot be applied automatically to the projection of future trends. An analysis of your institution's long-range plans will be needed to determine whether future growth is an extension of, or divergence from, past experience.

Part-time faculty as a percentage of all faculty describes the proportional representation of part-time faculty at your institution. The present model is based on faculty headcounts, although an FTE percentage could be developed instead. Again, the extent to which your institution has relied on part-time faculty in the past may not be indicative of future patterns. Institutions may also define "part-time" in a number of ways (e.g., by including administrators who teach) or have multiple "not full-time" categories in their model.

The percentages in **Table 3** represent averages over some or all of the individual years listed in **Table 1**. Multi-year averages are generally more reliable than single-year figures, thus producing more stable input for the projection model. Conversely, it may also be helpful to plot trend lines for selected data. Have rank proportions been shifting gradually over time, or do they vary cyclically? Has your institution's reliance on part-time faculty been increasing or decreasing of late? Have promotion and retirement rates been steady or erratic? The answers to these and other questions may provide insights that are obscured by multi-year averages.

INTERACTIVE MODELING

Interactive modeling allows decisionmakers to test alternative assumptions or hypotheses rapidly using a "live" spreadsheet at a meeting. The major advantage of such an approach is efficiency. In contrast to the presentation of a limited number of scenarios in a written report, interactive modeling allows for almost infinite flexibility in examining the projected impact of many different assumptions. This is especially true of faculty flow modeling, where the level of uncertainty associated with many of the contributing factors is typically high.

One practical benefit of interactive modeling is that the researcher need not be sent repeatedly back to the "drawing board," and decisionmakers need not hold multiple meetings to review the output of analyses. The time and cost savings can be considerable, especially for models with many variables and a wide range of expected values.

A related reason for recommending interactive modeling is its ability to simulate the probable consequences of institutional policy changes. For example, if a college takes action to reduce the attrition of junior faculty, the short- and long-term impact on faculty needs could be substantial and could have major implications for hiring strategies and resources. By having a model display an entire gradient of change (including either the gradual phasing-in of a new policy or procedure, or its immediate implementation), the researcher moves beyond the analysis of environmental contingencies to the much richer and more realistic field of institution-environment transaction.

Interactive modeling is not without its drawbacks, however. Electronic spreadsheets have perhaps too readily enabled researchers to develop models that are superficially

The historical data analyses provide useful descriptive profiles of your faculty in the recent past and some of the percentages to be used in the projection model. Remember that historical data should be updated with current information as it becomes available.

Projection Model

A number of probability models are available for the analysis of your data (see WICHE, 1992, for a discussion of statistical models used to project faculty demand). The more sophisticated models are based on complex probability matrices and entire faculty population distributions and are especially useful for large institutions or systems. Other models, including the example presented in **Table 4**, are more modest in scope and seem more appropriate for small institutional research offices and small- to medium-sized institutions. Both types of models yield estimates rather than actualities, and both suffer some degree of measurement error. It may be prudent to "start small," to validate and revise your model as needed, and then to expand it if the data and analytical resources are available. Finally, if you would prefer to explore an "off-the-shelf" projection model, you might consider the Consortium on the Financing of Higher Education (COFHE) Faculty Planning Package (Biedenweg & Keenan, 1989).

Table 4 combines faculty characteristics data with faculty flow percentages to produce projected faculty hiring needs. The total

sophisticated and convincing yet fundamentally unreliable. No model is any better than the data and assumptions that fuel it; computational speed and elegant graphics can create an illusion of validity that only the most careful objective scrutiny can recognize. In politically volatile situations, this risk is especially acute. A desired outcome may be used to justify the fabrication of those assumptions that will produce it. Rigorous institutional research must distinguish between dependent and independent variables and build models that produce conclusions from data rather than data from conclusions.

A parallel but more practical problem with interactive modeling involves the researcher's loss of control over the information flow. Once decisionmakers begin to tinker freely with the model, it can be difficult for the institutional researcher to regain control over the situation. There is also the risk that counterproductive or even absurd conclusions could be reached by pushing the model beyond its limits. For example, a faculty flow model that has lost its context or direction might lead one to conclude that the abolition of tenure, or the elimination of the assistant or associate professor ranks, is the single best way to avert a faculty shortage in the years ahead. Clearly, the larger mission and values of the institution and its faculty should set limits within which projection modeling must operate to be useful.

It is often helpful for institutional researchers to review the limits of their model and the ground rules for its use before an interactive session to discourage even benign abuse before it has a chance to occur. Interactive modeling is best seen as exploratory rather than definitive in nature. Unfortunately, it can be difficult to rein in decisionmakers once they have been mesmerized by the power and beauty of the statistical images that models produce.

number of faculty in each rank is derived by adding in-promotions and new hires and by subtracting retirees, nonretirement exits, and out-promotions from the base year. A separate table could be prepared for each department at your institution, although the same **Table 3** percentages would be applied to each (unless your institution has reliable faculty flow

For discussions of faculty demand projection models, see:

Biedenweg, R., & Keenan, T. (1989). *The COFHE faculty planning package — The faculty cohort model.* Cambridge, MA: Consortium on the Financing of Higher Education.

Daigle, S.L., & Rutemiller, H.C. (1989). *Projecting future faculty needs: A computer simulation model of nineteen campuses.* Paper presented at the 29th annual forum of the Association for Institutional Research, Baltimore, MD.

Table 4
Faculty Needs Projection Model

Year	1992	1993	1994	1995	2004	2005
Full Professor						
Total Faculty	24	24	25	26	18	19
Retirees	2	1	1	2	3	2
Other Exits	3	3	3	3	2	2
Total Exits	5	4	4	5	5	4
Promoted In	3	3	3	3	4	4
Associate Professor						
Total Faculty	25	26	27	28	33	35
Total Exits	9	9	9	10	11	12
Promoted In	7	7	6	6	8	8
Assistant Professor						
Total Faculty	28	28	27	26	35	33
Total Exits	12	12	12	11	15	14
All Ranks						
Total Faculty	77	78	79	80	86	87
Total Exits (Net)	16	15	16	17	19	18
Growth Hires	1	1	1	0	1	0
Total New Hires	17	16	17	17	20	18
New Hires by Rank						
Full	2	2	2	2	2	1
Associate	3	3	4	3	5	4
Assistant	12	11	11	12	13	13

Note: The figures in this table were not derived from those in previous tables.

percentages for different departments).

It should be emphasized that the accuracy of the projection model is only as good as the data and assumptions that enter it. Monitoring and revision of the model will be necessary as new data become available. Under the best of circumstances, the model describes future probabilities based on past experiences. It is an imprecise planning tool but offers direct and indirect benefits that, in combination with cautious interpretation, make the exercise worthwhile.

COMMUNICATION

The use of faculty supply and demand models will enable you to quantify, centralize, and standardize the analysis of faculty flow patterns at your institution. Initially there may not be many surprises in the data. Most astute deans and department chairs will have noticed, at least informally, the trends revealed by your model. Anecdotal impressions can be deceiving, however, as they are distorted by memory limitations and observer biases. The isolation and turnover of academic administrators are also sources of error. For example, the flow of faculty in one discipline at one point in time may be quite different from that experienced in another discipline or at another point in time. A quantitative model brings order, however imperfectly, to the sometimes serendipitous world of human resource management.

The advantages of formal models aside, results from your model will be used to inform decisionmakers, not to make their decisions for them. Deans and department chairs can benefit from your data, but your data can also benefit from their validation. Their feedback can raise some critical questions: Are you measuring the right things? Are there blind spots in the data that experienced academicians can identify? Are there artifacts hidden in even a 10- or 20-year trend line? The validators will also add important qualitative information to your data stream, linking trends to recommendations for action.

The results of your study will be used to inform two audiences: policymakers and resource allocators on the one hand, and human resource managers and academic personnel administrators on the other. The specific titles and hierarchy of individuals fulfilling these roles will vary from institution to institution. In general, policymakers and resource allocators will be more interested in long-range planning concerns, while human resource managers and academic and administrative personnel will be interested in hiring the right number of highly qualified candidates in any given search cycle.

Questions that your data can address for policymakers and resource allocators may include the following:

- What policies and practices at this institution can be changed to enhance the retention of current faculty and the successful hiring of new faculty? What makes this a more, or less, attractive workplace for a faculty member?

- What types of management efficiencies and mission shifts will be necessary for this institution to maintain or enhance its faculty in the years ahead? To what degree will faculty hiring challenges compel us to change and to take risks? In particular, how might resource allocation be managed differently to answer these challenges?

- What can this institution do to increase the supply of prospective faculty into graduate programs, enhance throughput within that system, and encourage new doctoral recipients to pursue faculty careers?

Questions that your data can address for human resource managers and academic personnel administrators may include the following:

- When will the demand for new faculty increase, and in which disciplines? How do our institutional needs match up with national supply and demand figures?

- In the event that demand for full-time faculty at this institution exceeds the number of qualified candidates that we are likely to hire from primary or traditional sources, what secondary or nontraditional sources are available as alternative or at least interim solutions?

- What types of cooperative ventures can this institution undertake to share faculty resources with other similarly stressed institutions?

REMEMBER

The projections from any faculty flow model are neither fixed nor magical. They simply tell what might happen if recent trends continue with current faculty. Changes in trends and/or in the composition of future faculty can have a tremendous impact on the accuracy of the model's output.

Even if you or others at your institution already have a good intuitive feel for future faculty hiring needs, a faculty supply and demand study offers a number of secondary benefits. These include rich descriptive information about the faculty, and past hiring and turnover patterns, which is not usually obtained in other reports. This information can be used to confirm or refute both common wisdom and the results of other studies. In other words, regardless of the projections themselves, you can learn things about your faculty and the professoriate nationally that may lead to new perspectives, strategies, and plans in a variety of areas. One might even argue that the greatest outcome of faculty demand modeling is idea generation, not quantitative forecasting.

This chapter does not address the issue of diversity in the hiring, management, and nurturance of tomorrow's faculty. This set of issues is examined in another chapter of this *Primer*. It should be emphasized, however, that the anticipated increases in faculty turnover in the years ahead may provide an opportunity for institutions to achieve a higher level of diversity at a faster pace than has been possible for the past 20 years.

Although national supply projections for racial/ethnic minority faculty in the next decade are not yet encouraging, institutions must nevertheless recognize this opportunity and develop creative initiatives to take advantage of it.

Faculty Salaries

Richard D. Howard, Julie K. Snyder, and
Gerald W. McLaughlin

ISSUES

Attracting and retaining good faculty is critical in maintaining institutional quality and strength. Institutional researchers help by providing information on the fairness and competitiveness of faculty salaries. Specifically, your analysis should address three fundamental questions:

- Do faculty at your institution earn salaries consistent with discipline peers at other institutions? In other words, are salaries *competitive*?

- Do salaries of new faculty approach or exceed salaries paid senior faculty in the same discipline? In other words, is there *salary compression*?

- Do protected classes, such as women and minorities, earn salaries that are consistent with

the majority? In other words, are salaries *equitable*?

Many factors influence faculty salaries, producing differences that are acceptable and, sometimes, unacceptable. Internal and external labor markets, the institution's salary structure, cost of living, discipline differences, and other factors are important to understand and consider.

Another often overlooked component is fringe benefits. Contributions to health insurance, liability insurance, retirement, and tuition benefits are several of the components of a standard fringe benefits package. The fringe benefits package offered by an institution is often 20 to 30 percent of the salary and varies significantly by institution. Fringe benefits represent a significant expenditure for the institution and can have a major impact on a faculty member's decision to work for your institution. While the focus of this chapter is salary analysis, you may need to look at issues of fringe benefits in designing many of your analyses.

This chapter focuses on the data and analysis issues for conducting institutional faculty salary studies. We present ways of addressing the questions of *competitiveness, compression,* and *equity.*

Julie K. Snyder is the assistant director of Institutional Research at Virginia Polytechnic Institute and State University.

Richard D. Howard is the director of Institutional Research at the University of Arizona. He was chair of the 1989 AIR annual forum.

Gerald W. McLaughlin is the director of Institutional Research at Virginia Polytechnic Institute and State University. He is a past president of AIR.

BACKGROUND

Research and literature on faculty salaries centers around three critical factors: *markets, structure,* and *cost of living.* Included in this literature are discussions of the influence of additional factors, such as discipline, workload, and personal variables.

Salary Markets

Breneman and Youn (1988) found that faculty salaries are influenced by multiple, overlapping labor markets. These labor markets generally can be categorized as internal or external to the institution.

Internal labor markets operate within an organization, individual campus, university system, or educational union and value key disciplines, stable employment, and promotional hierarchies. Although an internal market offers benefits beyond total compensation, employees are at risk of being recruited away if the internal compensation package is not competitive with the external market.

External labor markets involve the industry and tend to price and allocate labor on the basis of economic relationships, such as competition. The three main components around which external labor markets form are: teaching, research, and extension. The importance of these components in determining salary varies by institution. Similar institutions tend to compete in the same labor market. Additional factors, such

as size, location, and racial/ethnic diversity, influence the formation of submarkets. Teeter and Brinkman, in their chapter on institutional peer selection in this *Primer,* describe the relationship of some of these factors in institutional peer selection.

Sources on the factors influencing salary and salary markets include:

McLaughlin, G.W., Smart, J.C., & Montgomery, J.R. (1978). Factors which comprise salary. *Research in Higher Education, 8*(1), 67-82.

Breneman, D.W., & Youn, T.I.K. (Eds.). (1988). *Academic labor markets and careers.* Philadelphia: The Farmer Press.

Hansen, W.L. (1988). Merit pay in structured and unstructured salary systems. *Academe, 74*(6), 37-47.

Blum, D. (1989, October 18). Colleges worry that newly hired professors earn higher salaries than faculty veterans. *The Chronicle of Higher Education, 36*(7), A1, 21.

Keister, S.D., & Keister, L.G. (1989). Faculty compensation and the cost of living in higher education. *Journal of Higher Education, 60*(4), 458-474.

For the Higher Education Price Index, see:

Inflation measures for schools and colleges. (1991). Research Associates of Washington, 2605 Klingle Rd., NW, Washington, DC 20008. Phone: 202/966-3326.

Salary Structure

The faculty salary structure at an institution or system influences salary. Hansen (1988) describes this structure as a continuum with two extremes. At one end of the continuum is a very structured system where salary is determined solely by seniority and rank and, in some cases, by degree level. At the other end is a pure merit system. Most salary systems for faculty are a hybrid of these two systems. While more structured systems are viewed as fair, systems based on merit tend to attract and retain stronger faculty. However, a side effect of a merit system is greater internal variation in salary. Because of the subjective nature of measuring merit, there is always controversy over who judges merit and how it is measured.

Cost of Living

Keister and Keister (1988) found cost of living to be a significant factor in the competitiveness of faculty salaries. This factor is difficult to quantify for institutions located outside major metropolitan areas. One way to deal with local and regional differences is to consider cost of living when selecting institutional peers. Another method is to adjust the salaries at each institution by a local cost-of-living index or other index, such as the Consumer Price Index (CPI) or the Higher Education Price Index (HEPI).

Other Factors

McLaughlin, Smart, and Montgomery (1978) found differences in salary as a result of workload, discipline, rank, and personal characteristics, such as gender, race/ethnicity, and years of experience. All of these are potentially significant factors and should be considered in your analysis.

DATA

Data requirements vary depending on the issue analyzed. Data sources are both *external* and *internal* to your institution.

External Data

External data requirements usually include comparison data from institutions considered to be peers. This type of data is used in analyzing questions of salary competitiveness. For state and

> Sources on national faculty salary data include:
>
> *Faculty salary survey by discipline.* Office of Institutional Research, Oklahoma State University, Stillwater, OK 74078-0077. Phone: 405/744-6897.
>
> *National faculty salary survey by discipline and rank in state colleges and universities.* American Association of State Colleges and Universities and College and University Personnel Association, in conjunction with Appalachian State University, Boone, NC. Available from CUPA National Faculty Salary Surveys, Appalachian State University, Boone, NC 28608. Phone: 704/262-2124.
>
> *Academe, Bulletin of the American Association of University Professors.* Every year the March-April issue is a special issue called the "Annual Report on the Economic Status of the Profession." American Association of University Professors, Ste. 500, 1012 14th St., NW, Washington, DC 20005. Phone: 202/737-5900.
>
> Lenth, C.S., & Christall, M.E. (1991). National data bases and statistical resources on higher education: An annotated guide. In C.S. Lenth (Ed.), Using national data bases. *New Directions for Institutional Research, 69,* 83-107. San Francisco: Jossey-Bass.
>
> Education, Culture, and Tourism Division, Education Subdivision, Postsecondary Section, R.H. Coats Building, Holland Ave. and Scott St., Tunney's Pasture, Ottawa, Ontario, Canada K1A0T6. Phone: 613/951-1525.

land-grant colleges and universities, Oklahoma State University publishes average salaries by rank within discipline and region. The College and University Personnel Association (CUPA) collects salary and other demographic data on

Table 1

Examples of Internal Faculty Data Elements

Experience	Activity
Time in rank	Research grants
Time since degree	Teaching load
Time at institution	Publications
	Administration
	Extension
Salary	**Demographic**
Current salary	Gender, age, race/ethnicity
Starting salary	Degree (level, date, source)
Merit increases	Rank (current, starting)
Cost-of-living increases	Tenure data
	Full-time/part-time

faculty and administrators at both public and private institutions. *Academe* annually publishes average salaries by rank and institution using the Carnegie classification system. However, the *Academe* survey only collects data on average salaries at the institution level. Unfortunately, the discipline-level data available are not identifiable by institution. If you need discipline data for your peers, you may be faced with collecting the data yourself. Faculty salary information on Canadian colleges and universities is collected through the University and College Academic Staff System (UCASS) by the Postsecondary Education Section of Statistics, Canada.

Internal Data

The salary data elements stored in your institution's human resources system are typically the variables you use in analyzing issues such as salary compression and equity. These variables include experience, activity, salary, and demographics. **Table 1** categorizes the internal data elements that many institutions collect. If you need a variable that is not in your institution's database, you must collect the information directly. Usually, this involves a survey.

ANALYSIS

There are many approaches to analyzing salary. The disciplines of management, economics, law, sociology, public affairs, and statistics all contribute to the methods of salary analysis in higher education. The important point to recognize is that a single best method does not exist. As with all forms of analysis, the method is only applicable to a given set of circumstances. It is

Table 2

Average Management Department Salaries Compared to Peers

Rank	Institution	Peers	Difference
Professor	$56,770	$50,757	+$6,013
Associate Professor	$41,815	$40,172	+$1,643
Assistant Professor	$33,340	$31,876	+$1,464
New Assistant Professor	$38,000	$32,666	+$5,334
All Ranks	$44,525	$42,336	+$2,189

important that you select the appropriate method for your case and avoid drawing conclusions beyond the power of the method chosen.

Are Salaries Competitive?

Strategies to help ensure that salaries are competitive in national markets, or in a particular sub-market, range from simple to complex. Complex models often incorporate market conditions into the salary structure. Simpler models annually track average salary data to verify that a given discipline is ranked appropriately among its peers. Botsch and Folsom (1989) cite an example of a complex model at a small public institution. Here, the salary structure is based on a model where merit, market inequity, and time in service count toward the actual salary increase.

The California Postsecondary Education Commission (1990) lays out specific procedures to ensure that faculty salaries at the University of California and the California State University system are equitable and competitive. Criteria for selecting comparative institutions are identified, as is the methodology, for determining the salaries to be paid.

A starting point for determining whether salaries at your institution are competitive is to compare the average salaries by discipline and rank at your institution to the average salaries paid by peers. **Table 2** illustrates how this type of comparison may be presented. The data in the table reveal that full professors and new assistant professors in management make considerably more than their discipline peers. However, faculty

Table 3

Average Assistant Professor Salaries Compared to Peers

	Salary	Rank	COL* Rank
Institution A	$45,000	1	5
Institution B	$43,000	2	4
U. of Excellence	$41,000	3	7
Institution C	$39,000	4	1
Institution D	$38,000	5	6
Institution E	$36,000	6	2
Institution F	$35,000	7	10
Institution G	$34,000	8	3
Institution H	$33,000	9	8
Institution I	$32,000	10	9
Institution J	$31,000	11	11

*Rank after adjusting for differences in cost of living (COL)

at each rank do very well compared to peers, unless the cost of living at the institution is significantly higher.

A simple way to consider cost of living in an institutional-level comparison with peers is presented in **Table 3**. In this example, the University of Excellence's average salaries for assistant professors ranks third among the peer set. After adjusting for cost of living, its placement drops to seventh.

These two formats are starting points in establishing your institution's position in the marketplace. To really begin to understand how competitive your institution is, collect information on the offers made to faculty that were accepted and declined. Some of these will be counteroffers made to retain continuing faculty as well as offers to new faculty. If it is possible, collect as much information as possible about the offers of other institutions. Remember that not

Sources on how to incorporate market factors include:

Botsch, R.E., & Folsom, D. (1989). Market inequity: Incorporating this critical element into faculty salary plans. *CUPA Journal, 40*(1), 37-47.

California Postsecondary Education Commission. (1990). *Faculty salaries in California's public universities, 1990-91* (Report 90-10). 1303 J St., Fifth Floor, Sacramento, CA 95814-3985. Phone: 916/324-4992.

all perks are included in the salary. Teaching load, research facilities, and travel funds are but a few of a long list of items found in the salary offers faculty receive today.

Is There Salary Compression?

Salary compression refers to the phenomenon where junior faculty members receive salaries that approach or exceed those of faculty at more senior ranks. As you might expect, salary compression results in faculty turnover, low morale, and less willingness to support institutional initiatives. Because salary compression is funda-

mentally an issue of supply and demand, Blum (1989) expects the shortages of doctoral graduates to increase, creating shortages in the marketplace.

A simple method for analyzing salary compression is to compute the ratio of salaries paid to junior faculty compared to those paid to senior faculty. These ratios can be calculated by dividing the average salaries of the junior faculty by the average salaries of the senior faculty. Any time the ratio approaches one, salary compression is a potential problem. These ratios can be compared across disciplines, departments, and colleges to determine where the most serious problems exist. **Figure 1** is an example of how comparative salary ratios can be graphed to provide a quick picture of the salary compression situation for three colleges.

In this example, College 3 is a college where salary compression may be a problem. The ratio in this

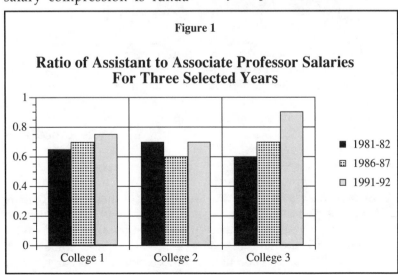

Figure 1

Ratio of Assistant to Associate Professor Salaries For Three Selected Years

Legend:
- ■ 1981-82
- ▦ 1986-87
- ☐ 1991-92

college steadily increased during the three years the ratio was computed, and is now 0.9. **Figure 1** suggests that the situations in College 1 and 2 are relatively stable, varying less over the three periods.

Compression ratios can be computed any number of ways to highlight specific areas of concern. For example, in **Figure 2** the focus is on departments rather than colleges. In this example, the question is not whether salary compression has increased over time but whether recent market assistant professors are rising. The ratios reveal that the salaries of assistant professors hired in the past two years are closer to associate professor salaries than to the salaries of those hired more than two years ago. This raises several questions: Will the assistant professors hired more than two years ago leave for higher salaries elsewhere? Should the institution recognize the shift in the market and adjust the salaries of the assistant professors with more than two years experience?

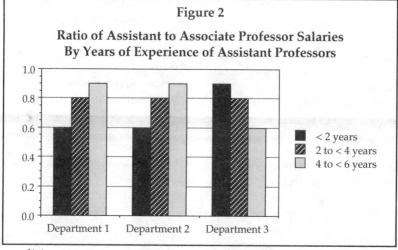

Figure 2

**Ratio of Assistant to Associate Professor Salaries
By Years of Experience of Assistant Professors**

conditions are causing salary compression in certain departments. This is accomplished by computing separate ratios for assistant professors based on their years of experience at the institution. As assistant professors' years of experience increase, average salaries should approach the levels of associate professors. This is the case with Departments 1 and 2, but not Department 3. The ratios in Department 3 may indicate that current market salaries for new

If this represents a permanent change in the market, will the department have sufficient resources to remain competitive in the future?

Although these procedures highlight areas of concern, you must look deeper. For example, if there are only a few salaries in a subgroup, the salary of one superstar may be enough to produce the illusion of salary compression. Also, some salary compression will occur if junior faculty are more aggressive than senior faculty at winning research grants and publishing. Because these factors may influence salaries at your campus, salary compression analyses are only an initial means to assess salary compression. Once an area is highlighted as a potential problem, care should be taken to review all factors that might account for salary differences.

Are Salaries Equitable?

There are many methods to judge the equity of the salaries of various groups. The simplest, of course, is a direct comparison. This can be done by using a t test for two independent groups. This method is not used often because the t test assumes the two groups have similar average salaries.

Typically, the assumption is that rational factors exist that cause the salary differences. Modeling the salary structure to explain the differences is accomplished by building an equation. Salary equity is modeled most frequently using a regression model. This statistical method is complex and easily biased. If you do not have a solid background in statistics and need to build a regression model, include a statistical expert from your faculty or administration in the design and interpretation of your findings.

Modeling Variables. There are many potential variables to include in a salary model. McLaughlin, Smart, and Montgomery (1978) studied the direct, indirect, and total influence of 39 variables as-

sociated with salary. They found rank and discipline to be major explanatory variables. Differences in faculty salaries between disciplines are considerable in both internal and external comparisons. In a survey of 18 disciplines in large, mostly public institutions, Hamermesh (1988) found a $25,000 difference between full professors in law and fine arts.

Rank and discipline are often used in regression analysis as moderator variables or as dummy variables. The tradeoff is that, if used as moderator variables, the groups may become too small for valid results. The problem with using these variables as dummy variables is that different disciplines have different reward structures.

A third useful variable is time-in-rank, or the number of years since promotion. This variable is best used with a quadratic term, but be sure to check if time-in-rank has a different relationship to salary for professors than for faculty at other ranks. All institutions tend to have senior faculty in ranks other than professor who are paid less than junior faculty.

Time-at-institution is sometimes a useful measure, as is time-since-terminal-degree. However, both variables tend to be correlated with time-in-rank, making it difficult to attribute effects to specific components. If used, use both variables with a quadratic term or after a logarithmic transformation. Be sure to check for nonlinearity.

Highest degree is a personal characteristic explaining salary differences at some institutions. Since the Ph.D. is not the terminal degree in disciplines such as dance and theatre, this variable must be used with caution. Other possible measures include tenure status, campus location (if multiple campuses exist), and type of appointment (academic year versus calendar year).

Faculty activity may also influence salary. There is evidence that time spent on various types of activities is rewarded differentially, depending on the academic discipline. In some institutions, differences in salary may increase depending on how much a faculty member teaches. However, this relationship may be inverse at some research institutions where teaching is related to lower salaries. Yuker (1984) gives a comprehensive description of some of the alternatives and complexities of measuring faculty effort. Your philosophical issue is deciding the degree to which your institution rewards various types of effort and the quality of that effort. Your empirical issue is the degree to which you can develop valid measures for these variables.

Finally, administrative position, such as that of a department chair or dean, may be useful in explaining salary differences. If some of these positions are rotating assignments at your institution, they probably will explain less of the salary differentials than if the appointments are permanent.

Methodologies. There are several regression-based methods to analyze salary equity between groups. The most popular method regresses a large number of variables on salary and then tests to see if the addition of group membership (e.g., gender or race/ethnicity) significantly increases the ability of the regression to explain the observed salary differences. However, if women or minorities are discriminated against, including them in the model may misspecify or invalidate the model. This concern led

---

References on variables for regression analysis include:

Yuker, H.E. (1984). *Faculty workload: Research, theory, and interpretation.* (ERIC Document Reproduction Service No. ED 259 691)

Hamermesh, D.S. (1988). Salaries: Disciplinary differences and rank injustices. *Academe, 74*(3), 20-24.

---

to the development of the best-White-male-model, in which the regression was developed using the characteristics of White males alone. Salary predictions are made for each group in the study (e.g., women and minorities) based on the male model and compared to actual salaries. Problems arise with this approach if males occupy a unique part of the salary distribution or if the relationship of salary to the male attributes is nonlinear.

The most common problem in interpreting a regression model is the extent of collinearity between group membership and the other measures related to salary. For example, when women tend to be in the humanities and social science disciplines and men in engineering, science, and business, collinearity can be a serious problem with gender and discipline variables. This situation results in the regression weight for gender or race/ethnicity appearing to account for some of the salary variation that could be explained by other independent, and perhaps more appropriate, variables. We recommend regressing salaries without a gender variable in the model then comparing the residuals of women versus those of men.

As you can see from this discussion, analyzing salary equity using a regression model is by no means a "scientific process." Le-

> **For discussions on regression analysis, see:**
>
> McLaughlin, G.W., Zirkes, M.B., & Mahan, B.T. (1983). Multicollinearity and testing questions of sex equity. *Research in Higher Education, 19*(3), 277-284.
>
> Rosenthal, W., & Yancey, B.D. (Eds.). (1985). The use of data in discrimination issues cases. *New Directions for Institutional Research, 48.* San Francisco: Jossey-Bass.
>
> Moore, K.M., & Johnson, M.P. (1989). The status of women and minorities in the professoriate: The role of affirmative action and equity. In G.G. Lozier & M.J. Dooris (Eds.), Managing faculty resources. *New Directions in Institutional Research, 63,* 45-63. San Francisco: Jossey-Bass.

gal and political considerations abound, and what variables are included in your model and how the model is analyzed can influence your findings. When you build a regression model, make sure your variables are well specified and differentiate the salaries at your institution. Once you have this in place, use the simplest appropriate statistical technique to analyze your variables.

COMMUNICATION

Faculty salary issues are one of the most sensitive questions institutional researchers analyze. Communicating the results of your work can be viewed from two perspectives: (1) what you share with decisionmakers and (2) what is released to constituencies within and without your institution.

Communicating your analysis to decisionmakers is a continuous process. The decisionmakers using your information should be involved in deciding the methods, variables, and format of your findings. This is especially important if a complex method of statistical analysis is utilized. If you follow this strategy, your decisionmaker often will explain to others not involved what your analysis means.

If your analysis is designed for public release, follow these simple guidelines:

- *Aggregate your data.* Do not release data into the public domain that points to an individual or a specific unit. For example, when analyzing salaries at the department level, aggregate data to the discipline (e.g., social science, letters, business, engineering).

- *Simplify your methods.* Communicate your methods so that someone unfamiliar with the statistics will understand your basic approach. Avoid using terminology that only statisticians understand.

• *Give weight to the conclusions.* The implication of your analysis for the institution is the most important aspect of your work. Although you must present the methods and variables used, make the issues and conclusions the centerpiece of what you communicate.

REMEMBER

Your faculty's sensitivity and attention to salary analyses will surface quickly, especially when the provost or president is presented a study that indicates that one group or another is paid above or below the norm. Defending your analysis is easier if you keep the following in mind when designing and conducting the analysis:

• *Use existing benchmarks to validate procedures and to select variables.* The literature, previous studies done at your institution, and studies at peer institutions provide benchmark parameters to use in comparing the results of your study.

• *Understand and define the basis upon which salary decisions are made at your institution.* If your salary system is merit based, what components of the faculty workload impact performance evaluations, and how should workload be measured? If your salary system is structured, identify the characteristics that define the structure.

• *Check the appropriateness of the analysis procedures in terms of the variables analyzed and your situation.* A frequency distribution of salaries within each of the cells is usually sufficient for structured salary systems. For merit systems, a more complex method is needed, probably involving a regression model. The best advice is to use the simplest solution that answers the questions at your institution.

• *Present the results in a way that clearly illustrates the comparisons examined in the analysis.* The object is to communicate clearly the situation to your decision-maker. Graphics and/or simple tables are the best format. Remember discussions of complex methodology detract from your findings.

• *Finally, discuss with faculty representatives the variables and procedures.* Listen to their concerns and advice; do not hesitate to meet with them to discuss the results or interpretation before going public. Making the faculty a knowledgeable part of the process enhances the acceptance of your analysis by the campus community.

Peer Institutions

Deborah J. Teeter and Paul T. Brinkman

ISSUES

Interinstitutional comparisons are often key factors in institutional strategic planning and decision-making. Comparative data provide managers with the ability to size up competition, act as benchmarks for assessing the well-being of their own institution, provide the ability to pinpoint areas deserving attention, and act as guides for policy development. Comparative data can also help explain and justify budget requests, salary increases, teaching loads, and tuition increases.

The success or failure of interinstitutional comparisons hinges upon the process of selecting peer institutions. This can be one of the most political processes with which the institutional researcher will have to deal.

In particular, to ensure that comparative data will serve your institution's intended purposes, the process of selecting comparison institutions is critical. You need to:

Deborah J. Teeter is the director of the Office of Institutional Research and Planning at the University of Kansas–Lawrence. She is a past president of AIR.

Paul T. Brinkman is the director of Planning and Policy Studies at the University of Utah.

• assess the overt and hidden political agendas surrounding the issues,

• understand the various types of comparison groups that can be constructed, and

• understand that the methodology used to select comparison institutions will, at some level, reflect the politics of the issue.

Selecting peer institutions can be one of the most political processes with which the institutional researcher will have to deal.

This chapter describes four types of comparison groups and some methods for developing peers for your institution. One methodology is described in detail. The chapter contains information about sources of data and other considerations in making comparisons.

BACKGROUND

The literature on peer institutions fits roughly into one of two categories: the broader conceptual work on the uses of peer comparisons and discussions of methodology for selecting peers.

Chapters in several issues of *New Directions for Institutional Research* provide good overviews of the conceptual issues. The 1989 volume "Enhancing Information Use in Decision-Making" provides broad discussions on the utilization of information as well as suggested ways for communicating information to decisionmakers. The 1987 volume "Conducting Interinstitutional Comparisons" includes chapters on sources of comparative data, setting up data-sharing projects, use of comparative data, comparative financial analysis, and effective interinstitutional comparisons. The political considerations of exchanging and comparing data are presented in a chapter in an earlier 1983 volume.

The literature on structural methodologies for selecting peers starts with the 1981 work by Elsass and Lingenfelter. Their work is cited frequently as exemplifying the use of multivariate statistics, such as cluster analysis, in identifying peers.

Subsequent literature details a number of approaches, including threshold and statistical models (Teeter & Christall, 1987) and clump analysis (McKeown & Moore, 1990).

COMPARISON GROUPS

Before you begin to select a comparison group, it is critical to understand the politics of using comparative data and to be knowledgeable about the various types of comparison groups. You will then be able to determine the most appropriate type of comparison group for the situation and purpose of the comparison.

> For overviews of the conceptual issues of comparisons, see:
>
> Teeter, D.J. (1983). The politics of comparing data with other institutions. In J.W. Firnberg & W.F. Lasher (Eds.), The politics and pragmatics of institutional research. *New Directions for Institutional Research, 38*, 39-48. San Francisco: Jossey-Bass.
> Brinkman, P.T. (Ed.). (1987). Conducting interinstitutional comparisons. *New Directions for Institutional Research, 53*. San Francisco: Jossey-Bass.
> Ewell, P.E. (Ed.). (1989). Enhancing information use in decision-making. *New Directions for Institutional Research, 64*. San Francisco: Jossey-Bass.

Politics of Using Comparative Data

Since comparative data are often used to justify, explain, or advocate a certain position, it is important to understand how the intended audience, whether internal or external to the institution, looks upon comparative data. Organizational and political realities need to be considered and a strategy developed accordingly. If the audience is likely to be hostile to the idea of using comparative data, it is imperative to involve them early in the game. Concerns often center on the validity of the comparison group. If that is likely to be the case, be sure to include the audience in the selection of the comparison institutions. It might serve to mitigate some of their concerns if they understand the rationale and criteria used to select the comparison institutions. Obviously, the data you draw upon should be accurate and easily understandable for the audience to properly assess the implications of the data.

For discussions of methodologies for selecting peers, see:

Elsass, J.E., & Lingenfelter, P.E. (1981). *An identification of college and university peer groups.* Illinois Board of Higher Education, 500 Reisch Building, 4 West Old Capital Square, Springfield, IL 62701.

Teeter, D.J., & Christall, M.E. (1987). Establishing peer groups: A comparison of methodologies. *Planning for Higher Education, 15*(2), 8-17.

Della Mea, C.L. (1989). *A comparison of two procedures for peer group assignment of institutions of higher education* (Doctoral dissertation, Virginia Polytechnic Institute and State University, Blacksburg, VA). Publication #8915719, University Microfilms, Inc., 1490 Eisenhower Place, P.O. Box 975, Ann Arbor, MI 48104.

McKeown, M.P., & Moore, N. (1990). *A new method for selecting peer institutions.* Paper presented at the annual meeting of the Rocky Mountain Association for Institutional Research, Missoula, MT. University Office of Institutional Analysis, Arizona State University, Tempe, AZ 85287-1203.

The key to the successful use of comparative data is properly sizing up the environment in which the data are to be used and taking the steps necessary to ensure that the audience will be receptive. Failure to lay the groundwork may result in extensive delay or prohibit the use of comparative data.

The Four Types

There are a number of different types of comparison groups, and all of them can play a legitimate role in informing decision-making, depending upon the situation. The issues to address will be important in choosing the type of comparison group. In an earlier publication, we identified four types of groups—competitor, aspirational, predetermined, and

peer. Furthermore, predetermined groups can be further differentiated as natural, traditional, jurisdictional, and classification-based.

A **competitor** group consists of institutions that compete with one another for students or faculty or financial resources. Although the institutions are competitors, they may not necessarily be similar in role and scope. For example, a shortage of faculty in a particular field, such as finance or accounting, may result in a four-year institution competing with a university for the same faculty. Depending upon the purpose of the comparison, the lack of similarity may or may not be important.

Comparison, by definition, means examining both similarities and differences, and examining differences is critical in developing an **aspiration** group. An aspiration group includes institutions that are dissimilar to the home institution but worthy of emulation. When a comparison group contains numerous institutions that are clearly superior to the home institution, the group reflects aspiration more than commonality of mission.

One word of caution in using aspiration groups: If they are presented as if they were peer groups, they can be costly in the political arena outside the campus. For example, if comparative data are used to buttress resource arguments, the masquerading of an aspiration group as a peer group may risk the credibility of most any comparative data the home institution wishes to use.

Figure 1

Four Types of Comparison Groups

Competitor	Aspiration	Predetermined	Peer
		natural	
		traditional	
		jurisdictional	
		classification-based	

It may fall to the institutional researcher to provide the reality check through assembling and presenting objective data on the alleged peers. If the appropriate data are chosen, the aspirational character of the proposed comparison group usually will be obvious. Still, individuals will ignore the obvious under certain circumstances, such as a no-holds-barred effort to increase funding, so the institutional researcher is advised to size up carefully where the comparative analysis fits in the overall institutional strategy. It cannot be stressed too much that the task of moving comparative data into the decision-making process is often more important than the technical routines for working with comparative data.

A **predetermined** institutional comparison group consists of institutions arranged together for some purpose outside of the institution. A predetermined group falls into one of four general categories: natural, traditional, jurisdictional, and classification-based.

Natural groups are those that are based on one or more of the following types of relationships: membership in an athletic conference, membership in a regional compact, or location in a region of the country. In effect, institutions already belong to a highly visible grouping of some sort, so it is natural to think of them as being comparable. They may indeed be comparable in some inherent sense, but the nature of your specific comparison is the critical test.

A *traditional* comparison group is one that is based on history. It has the advantage of being familiar and perhaps even enjoys wide acceptance. However, it may or may not be an appropriate comparison group in a given situation.

A *jurisdictional* group consists of institutions that are compared simply because they are part of the same political or legal jurisdiction. Frequently, the boundary for this type of group is the state line. Not surprisingly, elected officials and state agency staff will make comparisons of institutions within their purview, even though the institutions may have little else in common. Once again, the comparison issue in question is (or should be) the primary factor in determining the appropriateness of this kind of comparison group.

A *classification-based* group is one used for national reporting. Probably the best known is the classification developed by the Carnegie Commission in the 1970s and updated in 1987 (Carnegie Foundation for the Advancement of Teaching, 1987). The American Association of University Professors (AAUP) uses an institutional classification for reporting comparative faculty salaries (see the annual March-April issue of *Academe*). The U.S. government's National Center for Education Statistics (NCES) developed a classification of institutions for use in its *Digest of Educational Statistics* and *The Condition of Education*.

> Carnegie Foundation for the Advancement of Teaching. (1987). *A classification of institutional higher education: 1987 edition*. Princeton, NJ: Princeton University Press.

Using a classification-based comparison group saves time and effort. Further, the classifications have credibility and name recognition. The problem with the ready-made groups is that they typically are based on only a few comparative dimensions, such as size and the extent of research activity. As a result, they may contain too much within-group variation for certain types of comparative analysis.

A **peer** group consists of institutions that are similar in role and scope or mission. In this case, "similar" rather than "identical"

is the operative word. It is unrealistic to expect to find clones of the home institution unless the criteria for comparison are limited to categorical variables such as "public, land-grant, located west of the Mississippi." When interval variables are used to describe size, program content, or amount of research, it is unlikely that a perfect match between any two institutions will be found. However, "similar" institutions usually can be identified.

Developing a Peer Group

There are a number of procedures for developing peer groups. Options range from statistical approaches to those that depend entirely on judgment. **Figure 2** describes the typology of the most popular procedures. The top half of **Figure 2** describes the continuum of options and the bottom half indicates the techniques themselves (the techniques are meant to be a representative rather than an exhaustive list). Each of the techniques are briefly described in terms of the continuum and then an example of one of the procedures is provided.

Cluster analysis and supporting factor-analytic and discriminant techniques are characterized by heavy reliance on multivariate statistics and computer processing. An advantage of cluster analysis is that a large number of institutional descriptors can readily be handled. These statistical techniques tend to deemphasize the judgment of administrator input. The hybrid approach incorporates a strong emphasis on data and on

Figure 2
A Typology of Procedures for Developing Peer Groups

Emphasis			
Data & Statistics	Data & Statistics & Judgment	Data & Judgment	Judgment
Cluster Analysis	Hybrid Approach	Threshold Approach	Panel Review
Technique			

input from administrators, combined with statistical algorithms for manipulating data. The threshold approach also emphasizes a formal, systematic approach to data and to administrator input, but it depends little, if at all, on statistical algorithms. In the panel approach, administrator input is heavily emphasized; some data may be included informally but not systematically or comprehensively.

Threshold Approach

Various types of threshold procedures are available. One example is the approach developed and used by the National Center for Higher Education Management Systems (NCHEMS). The NCHEMS procedure combines raw data, thresholds, weights, and a modest statistical algorithm. The process utilizes both nominal variables, such as public versus private control, and interval variables, such as enrollment and the number of degree programs.

In the typical application, the nominal variables are used to reduce the universe of relevant institutions. For example, if "public control" is considered an essential characteristic for a potential peer institution, then any institution not publicly controlled is eliminated from further consideration.

After the nominal variables have been used to generate a subset of institutions, the interval variables are used to rank order the remaining institutions. Points are assigned to each institution based on the importance attached to each interval variable and the number of times an institution misses a prescribed range. Each miss on an important variable pushes the candidate institution down the list, further away from the home institution. The points are the basis for a rank order. The rank-ordered list is meant to be a guide for analysts and administrators at the home institution who make the final selection of institutions for their comparison group.

Table 1 displays a list of characteristics typically used by NCHEMS for four-year colleges and universities in selecting peers. The nominal variables (Set I) are used to

Table 1

NCHEMS Information Services

Criteria for Selecting Reference Institutions

(Four-Year Schools)

Name of your institution

Notes

Set I

| Items | Your institution | Check one | |
		Very important	Not important
Control (public/private)			
Landgrant			
Medical school			
Urban/rural			
Region (N. Atlantic/Gr. Lakes & Plains/Southeast/West & Southwest)			

Set II

| Items | Your institution | Range | Check one | | |
			Very important	Important	Not important
Total FTE students					
% Part-time headcount students					
% Bachelor's degrees					
% Master's degrees					
% Doctoral degrees					
% 1st-professional degrees					
# Bachelor's programs					
# Master's programs					
# Doctoral programs					
% Professional degrees					
% Academic degrees					
% Natural science degrees					
% Social science degrees					
% Humanities degrees					
% Health science degrees					
% Engineering degrees					
% Business degrees					
% Education degrees					
Research expenditures/instruction expenditures					
Research expenditures					

For questions, please call (303) 497-0319

All data provided by NCHEMS are from HEGIS/IPEDS files.

eliminate any candidate institution that does not meet criteria checked "very important."

The interval variables (Set II) are used to move institutions up or down on a list of possible comparison institutions. Ranges are established by the home institution; the frequency with which an institution falls outside of the home institution's ranges will place it further down the list. Additionally, a weighted score is calculated using the importance scale (a miss counts one point if the variable is "very important," one-half point for "important," and no points for an "unimportant" variable). The weighted sum is used to rank order the candidate institutions. Therefore, an institution's rank on a list of comparisons is a function of how well it fits the criteria and the weights assigned to those criteria. Based on the criteria established, a list of institutions is rank ordered by their "closeness" to the home institution.

Although the threshold approach provides an ordered guide, the selection of comparison criteria, weights, and ranges, as well as the final selection of peers, are all dependent upon the expert judgment of analysts and administrators. The procedure is designed to channel and highlight judgment based on data. The transparency of the procedure is a strength but it also can be a vehicle for manipulation. Manipulation can be countered only by designing appropriate checks and balances into the overall process of selecting a comparison group.

DATA

All the models for selecting comparison institutions require data, and there are several ways in which comparative data can be acquired:

- using *national databases*,

- joining a formal *data exchange* group that exists for the mutual benefit of participating parties, and

- collecting data on an *ad hoc* basis from selected institutions.

> For information on data bases and comparative data, see:
>
> Brinkman, P., & Krakower, J. (1983). *Comparative data for administrators in higher education: An NCHEMS executive overview*. National Center for Higher Education Management Systems, P.O. Drawer P, Boulder, CO 80301-9752.
> McKeown, M.P. (1989). State funding formulas for public institutions of higher education. *Journal of Education Finance, 15,* 101-112.
> Lenth, C.S. (Ed.) (1991). Using national databases. *New Directions for Institutional Research, 69.* San Francisco: Jossey-Bass.

National Databases

There are a number of national databases that you can consult to acquire data for selecting comparison groups. An annotated guide to these databases is contained in the Spring 1991 issue of *New Directions for Institutional Research*. The concluding chapter of the guide presents a method for categorizing national higher educational data and provides descriptions and sources for more than fifty national databases.

Data Exchanges

There are a number of formal data exchanges in higher education, and they can be used as sources of data if the policies and practices of the exchanges permit the sharing of data outside of those participating institutions. The Center for Planning Information located at Tufts University is a good source for those interested in information about existing data exchanges or interested in establishing formal data exchanges with other institutions.

> For information on data exchanges, contact:
> Center for Planning Information, Tufts University, 28 Sawyer Ave., Medford, MA 02155. Phone: 617/381-3808

The formal data exchanges typically make possible the sharing of more detailed and timely information than can be gained from public sources. Joint development of data formats, data definitions, and exchange procedures enhance the comparability of the shared data. Data exchange networks also have the advantage of cutting the number of redundant requests for data among institutions that are interested in the same type of comparative data. In addition, routine exchange through networks helps build longitudinal data for trend analysis. Formal exchanges often incorporate explicit guidelines for the use and sharing of the data, providing some assurance to participating institutions on the handling of their data.

Ad Hoc Collection

The collection of data on an ad hoc basis is probably the least desirable method. The time and effort needed for extensive data collection may very well exceed the value of the data collected. One issue is the difficulty in assuring comparability of ad hoc data. In addition, it is often difficult to motivate institutions to provide extensive information when the effort does not have tangible and immediate rewards. The exchange of ad hoc data for a particular issue may be viable, but it is not a good way to collect the kind of data typically used to select peers or other kinds of comparison institutions.

Limitations

The fundamental data concerns of validity, accuracy, and reliability are always present within a comparative context. Establishing how well these concerns are met is often more challenging when doing comparative analysis because comparative data are often derived from multiple sources. Also, the rules and definitions for recording such data may be inconsistent across sources, and the close familiarity that can be so helpful in spotting data errors is usually missing because one typically must depend on secondary sources.

The use and purpose of the comparison determines in part the extent to which errors of a given kind may compromise the comparison. For example, management-control situations may require highly accurate data, whereas data that are to be used in a strategic-planning context probably could be less accurate, in the sense of being precise, without causing problems.

REMEMBER

Institutional comparisons are best begun exactly where any good analysis begins—with a clear sense of purpose. With that in hand, one can address the technical and the human/political dimensions of the comparison process.

Both dimensions are important. On the technical side, the main area of concern is data. The act of comparing data from institutions other than your own compounds the typical data concerns of validity, accuracy, and reliability. The best approach is to proceed with caution, assuming as little as possible about the quality of the data. On the human/political side, although there are a number of procedures available for selecting

Institutional comparisons are best begun . . . with a clear sense of purpose.

comparison groups, you should choose one that suits your analytic skills, the purpose of the comparison, and the broader political aspects of your task. To get by politically, the procedure you choose must appear reasonable and valid to those who are to use its results. Involving interested parties in the process often helps, especially if the involvement is well managed and occurs early in the process

when the purpose of the comparison is being specified and the selection criteria are developing.

Even a solid analytic approach to selecting peer institutions in which the data and the selection methodology are carefully and thoughtfully chosen is no guarantee of success. Funding levels and institutional prestige, two of the most important issues for most colleges and universities, are often directly or indirectly affected by the development of peer groups. Thus analytical considerations are sometimes swamped by intense political struggles. This is especially likely to occur in the public sector, where funding, and perhaps even prestige, can sometimes be a zero-sum game.

In spite of the political struggles, the selection of comparison institutions and the use of comparative data continue unabated, as evidenced by the growth in the number of states using some form of peer groups. McKeown (1989) found just three states using some form of peer analysis to assess funding in 1984, but in 1988 the number had grown to 24. This finding underscores the importance of institutional researchers understanding the issues and various methodologies for selecting peers.

Diversity

Daryl G. Smith

ISSUES

Colleges and universities reflect the complexities in society's dealings with issues of diversity. Institutional researchers play a key role in these efforts. Effective research, however, requires an understanding of the broad issues as well as a sensitivity to the complex questions inherent in the institution's policies, priorities, and environment. This sensitivity and understanding impact institutional researchers in the following ways:

- *Framing the issues.* Increasingly, the focus of diversity analysis is turning *away from background characteristics* of students, faculty, administrators, and staff and *toward* study of *institutional factors* affecting success.

- *Designing and conducting effective analyses.* Institutional researchers designing research on diversity should focus on the success of the institution in meeting its diversity goals. These goals impact students, faculty and staff, campus climate, and curriculum. To con-

duct this analysis requires that researchers use multiple methods of evaluation and give careful consideration to the way they cluster groups, use standardized instruments, and focus their interpretations.

- *Communicating the results.* Research on diversity is by nature sensitive, prone to undetected bias, and open to multiple interpretations. As a result, institutional researchers must consider issues such as inclusivity, language, and categorizations *at the outset* of the diversity project. Also critical is inclusion of a diverse set of perspectives in the design of research and interpretation of the data.

This chapter focuses on the conceptual and design issues affecting institutional research on the diversity of students, faculty, administration, and staff. It provides a framework to use in improving your sensitivity and increasing your understanding of the broader context of diversity. In addition, it provides sets of key questions to guide your development of analyses of institutional success, participation of faculty and staff, campus climate, and educating for diversity.

Daryl G. Smith is associate professor of education and psychology at the Claremont Graduate School. She is author of The Challenge of Diversity: Involvement or Alienation in the Academy?

FRAMING THE ISSUES

For many years, discussion of diversity began, and often ended, with recognition that individuals from nontraditional populations came to college with different backgrounds, values, and preparation. This view established the institutional framework for dealing with students, faculty, and staff from many nontraditional populations. When the focus was on students, this translated into an assumption that students from nontraditional populations came with different levels of academic preparation, different values toward education, and different levels of sophistication.

In the familiar input-process-outcomes paradigm, this assumption focused almost exclusively on input and implied that process and expected outcomes were not in question. Under this assumption, research focused on the extent to which the new, nontraditional students diverged from the traditional norms of progress and outcomes. Researchers looked, for example, at the background of students who "succeeded" and compared it with those who did not. The assumption was the student's *background*, not the educational process, was responsible for success. As a result of this orientation, outcomes were usually in the form of strategies to produce conformity of the divergent student groups to the requirements of the traditional educational process.

Within this context, the focus of campus programs developed to assist students from nontraditional populations was on "remediation" and "institutional assistance." Such strategies included raising barriers, such as higher admission standards, shunting applicants to other institutions, or granting a provisional status to admitted students who required "remediation." Necessarily, then, the information gathered and analyzed was about student characteristics and not about the differential experiences of individuals or groups within the institution.

Increasingly, the focus of diversity analysis is turning toward study of institutional factors affecting success.

Today, higher education and society are taking a more encompassing view focused on the ability of colleges and universities to educate and prepare their students to live in a pluralistic society. The changing demographics in society and within colleges and universities certainly facilitate this shift. However, the shift is not the result of changing demographics alone. These changes are necessitated by weaknesses in higher education's record of success with underrepresented students and the increasing evidence of an alienating campus climate for underrepresented students.

The focus on the institution raises substantial questions about an institution's mission, its campus climate, and the ability of all members of the campus community to function in a pluralistic community. Central to this changing focus is the question: *What would our institution look like, and how would it function, if we were educating a diverse group of students for a pluralistic world and society?* In framing this question, the individual college or university moves away from analyses and programs fixed on the needs of specific groups and towards substantive study of the institution's capacity to organize and educate everyone within its community for a changing society.

Diversity vs. Quality

As the focus shifts to issues of institutional mission and function, fundamental conceptual tensions often emerge. A central tension is the supposed conflict between *diversity* and *quality*.

For background information on framing research questions, see:

Pace, C.R. (1984). *Measuring the quality of student experience.* Los Angeles, CA: University of California, Higher Education Institute. (ERIC Document Reproduction Service No. ED 255 099)

Blackwell, J. (1988). Faculty issues: The impact on minorities. *Review of Higher Education, 11*(8), 417-434.

Smith, D.G. (1989). *The challenge of diversity: Involvement or alienation in the academy?* (School of Education and Human Development Report No. 5). Washington, DC: The George Washington University Press.

Terenzini, P.T., & Pascarella, E.T. (1991). Twenty years of research on college students: Lessons for future research. *Research in Higher Education, 32*(1), 83-92.

Much of the energy devoted to the issue of diversity versus institutional quality focuses on lowered admission standards. Institutional researchers are involved frequently in designing studies related to diversity and lowered admission standards. Before developing these analyses, consider these three points:

- *Declining preparation of students is a national issue affecting virtually all schools and students.* Concern about inadequate preparation of students is **not** simply a minority problem.

- *There is nothing new about admissions policies that reflect differential levels of preparation.* Historically, even the most highly selective institutions sought geographic, athletic, artistic, and leadership diversity among their students. Admissions policies often reflected recognition that grades and test scores alone could not encompass all that is needed for success. Inherent in these policies was the presumption that institutional quality is made up of the contributions of those with varied talents.

- *Use of multiple achievement indicators in admissions considerations does not require lowering an institution's standards for learning.* Much of the tension between quality and diversity focuses on the lower than average scores of minority students on standardized tests. Yet, the predictive validity and power of these instruments are

> **Students**
> **Key Research Questions**
>
> - What is the demographic makeup of the student body in terms of race/ethnicity, gender, age, and other characteristics of importance to the institutional mission? How have the demographics changed over time?
> - What are retention and graduation rates for different student groups?
> - What are the satisfaction levels of students (and alumni) with the institution?
> - How do performance measures, such as grades, test results, courses taken, academic disciplinary fields, and levels of participation, differ for specific student groups?

often poor, especially for non-traditional students.

A common characteristic of successful colleges and universities is that they seek to admit students with varied strengths and talents, and then they provide the support students need to achieve. The focus of these institutions is on the effectiveness of their educational processes, not on the perceived inadequacies of incoming students.

DESIGNING DIVERSITY STUDIES

A focus on how well the institution's goals and processes serve diversity fundamentally alters both the kinds of research questions raised and the types of data collected on *students, faculty/staff, campus climate,* and *institutional mission.* In addition, it impacts how institutional researchers analyze the data and interpret the results.

Students

Data on students are perhaps the most central indicators of institutional success. While student success is obviously a result of the joint efforts of the student and institution, institutional factors strongly influence student performance. Indicators of student performance, then, are important in reflecting how well the institution has succeeded in attracting, retaining, and educating a diverse student body.

Faculty and Staff

Data on faculty and staff also are critical to measuring institutional success. Typically, the key underlying question is "Does the institution have role models to provide support to students from nontraditional groups?" While important, this question, again, looks only at the needs of specific student groups. However, the role of faculty and staff in achieving institutional diversity goals is much broader.

In institutions that are organizing for diversity, multiple perspectives are essential at all levels of decision-making and program development. However, the challenge of establishing diversity among faculty and staff is complex. To support these goals, the following information is needed on faculty and staff:

**Faculty and Staff
Key Research Issues**

- What is the diversity pattern among the faculty/staff?

- Are individuals of color and those from other nontraditional groups clustered in special programs and fields?

- What roles are persons from different groups playing in decision-making at the student, program, and institutional level?

- What are the levels of satisfaction and retention?

- What are perceptions about the fairness and adequacy of approaches toward recruitment, retention, and promotion?

- How central or marginalized do individuals from diverse groups feel in terms of involvement in decision-making and interaction on campus?

- How does the demographic makeup of the student body compare to the faculty and staff?

- *Analysis of the minority "pipeline."* Michael McGuire's chapter on faculty demand in this *Primer* outlines the issues and provides a guideline for institutional analysis and planning for faculty needs. As J. Blackwell (1988) noted, the inadequacy of the pipeline for faculty of color is one critical factor challenging successful diversification of key personnel in higher education. Too often, however, institutions may use this as an excuse to do nothing.

- *Identification of institutional problems.* Isolation, alienation, marginalization, and discriminatory practices limit the hiring and retention of a diverse faculty and staff.

- *Analyses of retention and development.* Identification of the factors influencing faculty and staff retention in the specific campus environment are critical to maintaining quality and diversity goals.

Campus Climate

Studying campus climate requires analysis of the *perceptions* of different campus groups. There is growing evidence that involvement in one's own education as well as a feeling of "connectedness" to the institution is an important predictor of success. As a result, studies that focus on the different perceptions of the campus by people of color, women, adult learners, gays and lesbians, and those with physical limitations have great importance.

Campus climate evaluation also needs to address the issues of conflict. Some degree of conflict is to be expected when individuals and groups interact in an institutional setting and attempt to create

---

Two key references on student involvement and success are:

Astin, A.W. (1985) Involvement: The cornerstone of excellence. *Change, 17*(4), 35-39.

Tinto, V. (1987). *Leaving college: Rethinking the causes and cures of student attrition.* Chicago: University of Chicago Press.

Campus Climate
Key Research Questions

- To what degree are students of different racial/ethnic groups involved in the life of the institution?

- What are the attitudes on campus toward interracial relations and contact?

- What are campus perceptions about the adequacy of the institution's response to incidents of discrimination and harassment?

- Do students feel that the institution values diversity and supports these goals?

- Do members of the community support goals for diversity?

- Are policies adequate for dealing with incidents of discrimination and harassment?

- Are there differential patterns of interaction among students from different backgrounds?

- Do students from different backgrounds perceive similar levels of encouragement and interaction with faculty?

- Do students feel that they have to lessen their identification with their own background to be successful on campus?

- Do adequate means exist to resolve disputes?

- Does the campus community recognize that differences exist?

- What is the level of conflict on campus?

- How adequate is communication at all levels of the institution and among diverse groups?

- Are there access problems on campus for those with physical limitations?

- Do the campus architecture, use of space, and art communicate a value of diversity?

- Is there an explicit or underlying assumption that diversity and quality are at odds?

- Do students feel that they are expected to succeed and are given support for succeeding, or that they are expected to fail?

---

a learning community. The classic intergroup relations literature suggests, moreover, that certain common conditions increase conflict: a competitive environment, unequal status of individuals and groups, frustration caused by hostile environments, perceptions of unresponsiveness by some and favoritism by others, and little focus for meaningful contact between groups.

Educating for Diversity

More and more colleges and universities are beginning to articulate commitment to educate all students for a pluralistic world. This commitment involves shaping the curriculum to include educating for diversity, changing teaching styles to enhance learning about diversity and to accommodate learning needs of diverse students, and finding ways to effectively assess outcomes of learning about diversity.

> **Guides and instruments for assessing campus climate include:**
>
> *Student climate issues.* (1982, 1984). Association of American Colleges, 1818 R St., NW, Washington, DC 20009. Phone: 202/387-3760.
> *Campus climate revisited.* (1986). Association of American Colleges, 1818 R St., NW, Washington, DC 20009. Phone: 202/387-3760.
> Green, M. (1989). *Minorities on campus: A handbook for embracing diversity.* American Council on Education, One DuPont Circle, Washington, DC 20036. Phone: 202/939-9380.
> *Assessment of Campus Climate* (Report 92-2). (1992). California Postsecondary Education Commission, 1303 J St., Fifth Floor, Sacramento, CA 95814-3985. Phone: 916/324-4992.

Values are also critical components in achieving institutional diversity goals and creating a climate that supports these goals. Perhaps the most challenging value conflicts occur when students perceive that their values and perspectives are not appreciated and may even conflict with institutional norms and behaviors. Students may perceive that they must abandon their own cultural values and adopt the prevailing values in order to succeed. Other tensions can emerge when an individual or group prefers cooperative relationships and learning in an institution that stresses individualism and competition.

The undergraduate curriculum is characteristically resistant to change; it becomes entrenched over time because faculty preparation for teaching courses originates in the doctoral program and is reinforced each time a faculty member teaches a familiar course. Under these circumstances, reorienting a course or developing a new one is a major undertaking. Further, control of curricular decisions rests firmly within each program area or department. Faculty build an allegiance to the content of the courses they offer year after year because they have invested so much of their professional lives in learning, honing, and continually updating the subject matter. To be persuaded that their courses are deficient or misguided unless they contain adequate emphasis on cultural pluralism is not an easy matter. Add to this the frequently voiced concerns about the politicization of curricular change, and it is easy to see how the institutional researcher needs to tread warily when asked to study the infusion of cultural pluralism in the curriculum.

The same caution is advised when studying teaching styles. In most colleges, the classroom is sacrosanct. Any suggestion that teaching styles are outmoded or inadequate unless they accommodate a relatively new emphasis on cultural pluralism will threaten or antagonize faculty not predisposed to accept this perspective. If any research plan by the institutional researcher to examine either course content or teaching style is perceived as more advocacy than objective assessment, it will be resisted—even by those predisposed to infuse cultural plurality into the curriculum.

Objectivity and recognition of faculty concerns about loss of control over the curriculum are integral to adequate assessment of how well the institution educates for diversity. Selection of types of assessment must recognize such concerns in order to be successful. Requests for course syllabi, study materials, interviews, administration of questionnaires, and especially access to classrooms should be made through proper academic channels. In many institutions, approval should be sought from faculty senates or other representative groups as well as from academic leadership, such as deans and program chairpersons.

Finally, the institutional researcher should be sensitive to the lack of consensus among students on most campuses regarding the desirability or need for an emphasis on cultural diversity. Students in professional majors, in particular, may perceive that any new emphasis will either displace curricular content needed to meet professional expectations in the field or will add to indispensable content and extend their academic programs further. Cultural diversity is a controversial issue on many campuses, and the institutional researcher should be aware that some student organizations will be as opposed to it on

ideological or political grounds as others will be for it. The key to successful research involving students is to engage these issues thoughtfully and to involve a wide enough variety of campus leaders to ensure support for the research.

GETTING STARTED

How does an institutional researcher handle the fact that diversity affects all levels of the institution and could require a research project that would consume years? **Figure 1** outlines a basic approach to developing an initial research project on diversity. The approach includes gathering information from major campus groups and using a variety of analytical methods; but, this approach is selective in terms of the focus of the questions to be addressed and the comprehensiveness of the methodologies used. As with any other research project, the campus will need to define specific questions to focus the data collection and to develop manageable information. Instruments, such as the Institutional Goals Inventory, also may be helpful in defining questions and providing data.

Figure 1
Steps to Developing a Diversity Research Study

Step 1 *Gather data* on student demographics, retention, and program participation from institutional records.

Step 2 *Survey a sample* of all students (or survey all students, if the student body is small enough), assessing student satisfaction, perceptions about the climate of the institution, attitudes about the institutional mission and their educational experience.

Step 3 *Interview students* from diverse backgrounds to assess very broadly their experiences on campus and their perceptions of the campus climate.

Step 4 *Gather alumni feedback* through a general survey or through focused discussions with a small sample.

Step 5 *Interview selected faculty and staff* concerning their experiences of the climate of the campus (valuable but optional depending on the need).

In addition, a number of studies by individual campuses include survey instruments. Stanford's *Final Report of the University Committee on Minority Issues*; the report from the Institute for the Study of Social Change at Berkeley, *The Diversity Project*; and the *Assessment of Campus Climate* and its related case book, developed by the California Postsecondary Education Commission, are all useful in developing a campus study and report. Other general instruments, such as the *College Student Experience Questionnaire* (see Pace, 1984), assess overall participation and satisfaction among different subgroups.

Data Sources

The research questions listed throughout this chapter lend themselves to a wide variety of data sources.

Archival Data. Student records, institutional data, and faculty records can be used to describe the institution's success in meeting its goals of access, performance, and retention of students, staff, and faculty. Data on the involvement of specific groups or the entire campus community might also be available from lists of those participating in student life programs and groups, alumni and board activities, and fundraising.

Annual Surveys. Annual surveys of students are common ways to get information on students' experiences and satisfaction.

For information and examples on survey instruments, see:

Final Report of the University Committee on Minority Issues. (1989). Office for Multicultural Development, Building 10, Stanford University, Stanford, CA 94305-2060. Phone: 415/723-3484.

The diversity project: Final report. (1991). Institute for the Study of Social Change, University of California at Berkeley, 2420 Bowditch St., Berkeley, CA 94720.

Institutional Goals Inventory, Institutional Functioning Inventory, and *Program Self-Assessment Service.* Educational Testing Service, Publication Order Service (TO-1), P.O. Box 6736, Princeton, NJ 08541-6736

Studies can be focused on class groups, those who stay and leave, seniors, residential life areas, fraternity and sorority groups, etc. Comparing the experiences and attitudes of students from all racial/ethnic groups and other nontraditional groups can indicate important information about differential experiences and interactions between and among them.

Alumni Surveys. Periodic surveys of alumni can provide reflective data about the experiences of former students and the degree to which they feel the institution was supportive of and focused on educating for diversity.

Interviews and Focus Groups. Interviews and focus groups (see Craig Clagett's chapter in this *Primer*) may reveal qualitative information about the campus climate, experiences among students, factors affecting success, and perceptions about the campus from different groups.

Diversity Analysis Issues

Using Standardized Test Results. The appropriate use of standardized test results in evaluating an institution's success in reaching its diversity goals is a thorny issue. On the one hand, new emphasis on assessment often pushes the use of standardized tests because of their availability and sophistication and because they permit relatively objective comparisons between individuals, programs, and institutions. On the other hand, there is increasing evidence that the predictive validity of the tests for minorities and women is weak.

There is evidence, for example, that there is a lower correlation between SAT scores and first-year grades for Latinos and women than for Whites and men. Recent court cases have ruled that exclusive reliance on SAT and ACT scores results in discrimination against women and minorities

> **For discussions of standardized tests and minority students, see:**
>
> Morris, L.W. (1981). The role of testing in institutional selectivity and black access to higher education. In G.E. Thomas (Ed.), *Black students in higher education: Conditions and experiences in the 1970s* (pp.64-75). Westport, CT: Greenwood Press.
>
> Verdugo, R.R. (1986). Educational stratification and Hispanics. In M.A. Olivas (Ed.), *Latino college students* (pp. 325-347). New York: Teacher's College Press.
>
> **An easy-to-use resource on stratification techniques is:**
>
> Bradburn, N.M., & Sudman, S. (1989). *Polls and surveys.* San Francisco: Jossey-Bass.

(*Chronicle of Higher Education*, February 15, 1989). The Educational Testing Service itself suggests that these instruments not be used as the sole source of information in college admissions and placement decision-making (*College Board News*, 1987, Summer, 15(4)).

Using Multiple Methods. Multiple methods and sources, such as surveys, case studies, and interviews, may be necessary in diversity studies to ensure that all factors related to student or faculty/staff experiences are considered. When combined with quantitative data, these more qualitative sources can provide powerful information.

Clustering Groups. In conducting diversity analyses, institutional researchers must be particularly sensitive to the way they cluster minorities into groups such as "Asian Americans" or "American

> For discussions of classification issues, see:
>
> Duran, R.P. (1986). Prediction of Hispanics' college achievement. In M.A. Olivas (Ed.), *Latino college students* (pp. 221-245). New York: Teacher's College Press.
>
> Carter, D., Pearson, C.S., & Shavlik, D. (1988). Double jeopardy: Women of color in higher education. *Educational Record, 69*(1), 86-103.
>
> Hsia, J. (1988). Asian Americans fight the myth of the super student. *Educational Record, 68*(4)-69(1):94-97.

Indians." The Census Bureau, for example, uses the "Hispanic" classification for grouping Mexican American, Puerto Rican, Cuban, Central American, and South American groups together. Yet, evidence shows very different experiences among these groups. The "Asian American" classification includes over 60 different ethnic groups, including Korean, Japanese, Cambodian, and Vietnamese.

Watching the Sample Size. Sample size is another problem in doing diversity research where the Ns for some groups are small. It is important to consider one of many oversampling techniques through stratification to assure valid representation of all groups in the analysis.

Focusing the Interpretation. As data are interpreted, you will want to ensure that the focus of attention is on the institution rather than on particular groups. For example, in evaluating the results of campus climate studies, it is common to hear observations that a particular student group isolates itself by eating together. The implication of this conclusion is that the problem is with the group. Such a conclusion ignores the fact that the alienation and hostility that exists on campus may explain the need for "safe havens" for students who are in a minority on campus. Moreover, it ignores the fact that students with common interests (e.g., football players, fraternity members) have always "hung out" together.

In studying turnover in faculty or staff, it is important to look at the ways the institution contributes to turnover through isolation, lack of communication, and inappropriate standards of evaluation. Inordinate demands on faculty and staff of color, including large advising loads, increased demands for committee work, and the challenge of being a minority at the same time that they are expected to meet and exceed normal expectations, are all contributing factors to be explored. Incidents of harassment add to the challenge.

COMMUNICATION

Because research on this topic is sensitive and prone to undetected bias, it will be important to involve a diverse advisory group in the design of the study and in the interpretation of the results. As much as possible, the group must develop an environment of trust so that those issues that can be informed better through research will be developed in constructive ways. Communication issues should be considered from the outset of the project. Involve the advisory group at all levels of the study so that critiques of methods cannot be as easily introduced after results are presented.

While all the good principles of practice apply here, there are a number of special issues that are important to address:

- *Inclusivity.* Consideration should be given to whether or not the focus of the analysis is primarily on racial/ethnic issues or whether the analysis should include gender, class, sexual orientation and/or physical and learning limitations as well. To include all groups may not give adequate voice to any one group. Yet, a focus on only one group gives rise on many campuses to a profound sense of being ignored by those left out. Diversity within the decision-making group will be important in dealing with inclusivity issues.

- *Language.* Insensitivity to how groups are named can impact the ways in which research will be received and interpreted. Today, terms like "African American" and "Latino" may be preferred, although different preferences evolve on different campuses. Increasingly, campus groups are concerned about the term "minority." This term implies a dichotomy concerning majority/minority status that is not true in the world, will shortly not be true in several states, and is no longer true on many campuses. Lack of respect for chosen names will affect the discourse and trust that results.

- *Single categorization.* Asking students or others on campus to self-identify with only one group will be increasingly offensive to those who come from mixed backgrounds. Those whose parents are of two different ethnic groups, for example, are essentially being asked to choose, something few wish to do. Creating options on surveys for multiple identification will suggest openness to the reality of people's lives and will reveal a willingness on the part of the institution to change.

- *Multiple methods.* The most successful reports on diversity combine quantitative data and qualitative data. These reports contain the quantitative responses to particular questions, coupled with qualitative information communicating more fully the reality of experiences on the campus. Deciding which anecdotes are needed and where hard data are needed is an important function of an advisory group. A focus on the institution can be instrumental in gaining support for the report and its recommendations from all groups.

REMEMBER

This chapter really is grounded in the many suggestions contained in other chapters on specific topics in this *Primer*. The researcher who begins to engage these issues now will be better prepared at the time a call is made for comprehensive studies or for existing data related to diversity.

The goal of research related to diversity is to provide a perspective on the ways in which the institution is or is not succeeding and how it can be more successful. The focus is on the *institution* and its educational success related to diversity.

Qualitative and quantitative methodologies described in this chapter are very useful in providing rich information that facilitates institutional assessment and discussion on this complex and sensitive topic.

Perhaps more than most areas of institutional research, however, this area requires that the institutional researcher participate as part of a diverse group or develop a design that engages diverse constituencies. The social and political implications of these issues require that the institutional researcher pay more attention to process than is usually the case. The opportunity is there for the institutional researcher to play an important leadership role.

The rhetoric and controversy about diversity makes it a very volatile topic. The role of research in this area is not to provide an answer to all of the issues, but to create an information base that will promote direct institutional self-evaluation and facilitate dialogue.

DIVERSITY

Environmental Scanning
James L. Morrison

ISSUES

Successful management of colleges and universities depends upon the ability of the senior leaders to adapt to rapidly changing external environment. Unfortunately, the lead time once enjoyed by decisionmakers to analyze and respond to these and other changes is decreasing. Traditional long-range planning models, with their inward focus and reliance on historical data, do not encourage decisionmakers to anticipate environmental changes and assess their impact on the organization (Cope, 1981). The underlying assumption of such models is that any future change is a continuation of the direction and rate of present trends among a limited number of social, technological, economic, and political variables. Thus, the future for the institution is assumed to reflect the past and present or, in essence, to be "surprise-free." However, we know that this is not true, and the further we plan into the future, the less it will be true.

James L. Morrison is professor of education in the Program in Educational Leadership at the University of North Carolina. He is editor of <u>On the Horizon</u>, the environmental scanning newsletter of higher education.

Editor's Note:

The Readers' Guide to Periodical Literature, published by the H.W. Wilson Company, is an index to English language periodicals of general interest available in most libraries. We consider a periodical to be readily accessible if it is indexed in the *Readers' Guide*. For those periodicals not included in the *Readers' Guide*, we provide the address and, in most cases, the phone number to guide you in your scanning.

The Encyclopedia of Associations, published by Gale Research, Inc., is a guide to over 22,000 national and international organizations. Information about how to contact the organizations mentioned in this chapter is from the 1992 edition of *The Encyclopedia of Associations* and is available in most libraries.

Publications of U.S. government agencies are indexed in the *Monthly Catalog of United States Government Publications*. Most publications included in the *Monthly Catalog* are available from The Superintendent of Documents, U.S. Government Printing Office, 732 N. Capitol St., NW, Washington, DC 20401. Information: 202/275-3648, orders and inquiries: 202/783-3238.

What is needed is a method that enables decisionmakers both to understand the external environment and the interconnections of its various sectors and to translate this understanding into the institution's planning and decision-making processes. *Environmental scanning* is a method of accomplishing this.

Brown and Weiner (1985) define environmental scanning as "a kind of radar to scan the world systematically and signal the new, the unexpected, the major and the minor" (p. ix). Aguilar (1967), in his study of the information-gathering practices of managers, defined scanning as the systematic collection of external information in order to (1) lessen the randomness of information flowing into the organization and (2) provide early warnings for managers of changing external conditions. More specifically, Coates (1985) identified the following objectives of an environmental scanning system:

- detecting scientific, technical, economic, social, and political trends and events important to the institution,

- defining the potential threats, opportunities, or changes for the institution implied by those trends and events,

- promoting a future orientation in the thinking of management and staff, and

- alerting management and staff to trends that are converging, diverging, speeding up, slowing down, or interacting.

Fahey and Narayanan (1986) suggest that an effective environmental scanning program should enable decisionmakers to understand current and potential changes taking place in their institutions' external environments. Scanning provides strategic intelligence useful in determining organizational strategies. The consequences of this activity include fostering an understanding of the effects of change on organizations, aiding in forecasting, and bringing expectations of change to bear on decisionmaking.

A number of writers on educational planning encourage college and university decisionmakers to use environmental scanning as part of their strategic planning models. This chapter reviews several environmental scanning models and discusses how environmental scanning is used in higher education. Also included are suggestions on establishing an environmental scanning process at your institution and a listing of useful scanning resources.

For overviews of environmental scanning, see:

Aguilar, F. (1967). *Scanning the business environment*. New York: Macmillan.

Cope, R. G. (1981). Environmental assessments for strategic planning. In N.L. Poulton, (Ed.), Evaluation of management and planning systems. *New Directions for Institutional Research, 31*, 5-15. San Francisco: Jossey-Bass.

Fahey, L., King, W.R., & Narayanan, V.K. (1981). Environmental scanning and forecasting in strategic planning: The state of the art. *Long Range Planning, 14*(1), 32-39.

Brown, A., & Weiner, E. (1985). *Supermanaging: How to harness change for personal and organizational success*. New York: Mentor.

Coates, J.F., Inc. (1985). *Issues identification and management: The state of the art of methods and techniques* (Research Project 2345-28). Electric Power Research Institute, 3412 Hillview Ave., Palo Alto, CA 94304. Phone: 415/855-2000.

Fahey, L., & Narayanan, V.K. (1986). *Macroenvironmental analysis for strategic management*. St. Paul, MN: West.

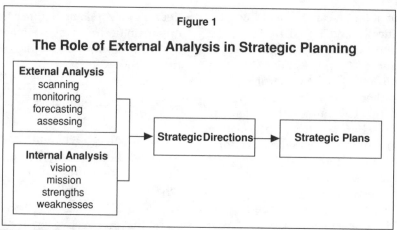

Figure 1

The Role of External Analysis in Strategic Planning

External Analysis
  scanning
  monitoring
  forecasting
  assessing

Internal Analysis
  vision
  mission
  strengths
  weaknesses

Strategic Directions

Strategic Plans

BACKGROUND

Environmental scanning is one of four activities comprising **external analysis**. As illustrated in **Figure 1,** external analysis is the broader activity of understanding the changing external environment that may impact the organization. In describing external analysis, Fahey and Narayanan (1986) suggest that organizations *scan* the environment to identify changing trends and patterns, *monitor* specific trends and patterns, *forecast* the future direction of these changes and patterns, and *assess* their organizational impact. Merged with **internal analysis** of the organization's vision, mission, strengths, and weaknesses, external analysis assists decisionmakers in formulating strategic directions and strategic plans.

The goal of environmental scanning is to alert decisionmakers to potentially significant external changes before they crystallize so that decisionmakers have sufficient lead time to react to the change. Consequently, the scope of environmental scanning is broad.

Defining Environment

When we scan, it is useful to view the environment in a manner that organizes our scanning efforts. Fahey and Narayanan (1986) help by identifying three levels of environment for scanning. The **task environment** is the institution's set of customers. In higher education, this may include students and potential students, parents of students and of potential students, political leaders, and employers and potential employers of students. The task environment relates to a particular institution. Although the task environments of a community college and a research university within 20 miles of each other may overlap, they also differ.

The **industry environment** comprises all enterprises associated with an organization in society. For higher education, factors such as public confidence in higher education or student aid legislation are industry factors affecting all institutions.

At the broadest level is the **macroenvironment,** where changes in the social, technological, economic, environmental, and political (**STEEP**) sectors affect organizations directly and indirectly. For example, a national or global recession increases the probability of budget cuts in state government and, consequently, budget reductions in publicly supported colleges and universities.

Defining Scanning

There are a number of ways to conceptualize scanning. Aguilar (1967) identified four types of scanning. **Undirected viewing** consists of reading a variety of publications for no specific purpose other than to be informed. **Conditioned viewing** consists of responding to this information in terms of assessing its relevance to the organization. **Informal searching** consists of actively seeking specific information but doing it in a relatively unstructured way. These activities are in contrast to **formal searching**, a proactive mode of scanning entailing formal methodologies for obtaining information for specific purposes.

Morrison, Renfro, and Boucher (1984) simplified Aguilar's four scanning types as either passive or active scanning. **Passive scanning** is what most of us do when we read journals and newspapers. We tend to read the same kinds of materials—our local newspaper, perhaps a national newspaper like *The New York Times* or *The Wall Street Journal*, or an industry newspaper like *The Chronicle of Higher Education*. However, the organizational consequences of passive scanning are that we do not systematically use the information as strategic information for planning, and we miss many ideas that signal changes in the environment.

Active scanning focuses attention on information resources that span the task and industry environments as well as the macroenvironment. In active scanning, it is important to include information resources that represent different views of each STEEP sector.

Another way of looking at scanning was described by Fahey,

For a discussion on environmental scanning in higher education planning, see:

Keller, G. (1983). *Academic strategy: The management revolution in American higher education.* Baltimore, MD: Johns Hopkins University Press.

Morrison, J.L., Renfro, W.L., & Boucher, W.I. (1984). *Futures research and the strategic planning process: Implications for higher education* (ASHE-ERIC Higher Education Research Report No. 9). Washington, DC: Association for the Study of Higher Education. (ERIC Document Reproduction Service No. ED 259 692)

Callan, P.M. (Ed.). (1986). Environmental scanning for strategic leadership. *New Directions in Institutional Research, 52.* San Francisco: Jossey-Bass.

Morrison, J.L. (1986-1987). Establishing an environmental scanning system to augment college and university planning. *Planning for Higher Education, 15*(1), 7-22.

Morrison, J.L., & Mecca, T.V. (1989). Managing uncertainty. In J.C. Smart (Ed.), *Handbook of theory and research in higher education: Vol. 5* (pp. 351-382). New York: Agathon.

King, and Narayanan (1981). Their typology views scanning as irregular, periodic, and continuous. **Irregular** systems are used on an ad hoc basis and tend to be crisis-initiated. These systems are used when an organization needs information for planning assumptions and conducts a scan for that purpose only. **Periodic** systems are used when the planners periodically update a scan, perhaps in preparation for a new planning cycle. **Continuous** systems use the active scanning mode of data collection to systematically inform the strategic planning function of the organization. The rationale undergirding active scanning is that potentially relevant "data" are limited only by your conception of the environment. These data are inherently scattered, vague, and imprecise and come from a host of sources. Since early signals often show up in unexpected places, your scanning must be ongoing, fully integrated within your institution, and sufficiently comprehensive to cover the environments important to your decisionmakers.

Scanning in Higher Education

Many colleges and universities incorporate environmental scanning in strategic planning. Friedel, Coker, and Blong (1991) surveyed 991 two-year colleges in spring 1991 to identify those institutions that currently conduct environmental scans. Based upon a 60 percent response rate, they found that 40 percent of the responding institutions conduct some form of environmental scanning. Of these institutions, 20 percent use an irregular system, 40 percent use a periodic system, and 32 percent use a continuous system. Meixell (1990), in a survey of 134 public research and doctorate-granting institutions, found environmental scanning activities in the planning processes at half of the institutions surveyed.

The best discussion of how postsecondary institutions implement environmental scanning is found in Pritchett (1990). Pritchett discusses how three institutions, a public doctoral-granting university, a comprehensive university, and a two-year college, use environmental scanning in the planning process. Two institutions use an ad hoc environmental analysis committee appointed by the president. At the other institution, the

For reports on scanning activity in colleges and universities, see:

Pritchett, M.S. (1990). *Environmental scanning in support of planning and decision-making: Case studies at selected institutions of higher education.* Paper presented at the annual forum of the Association for Institutional Research, Louisville, KY. (ERIC Document Reproduction Service No. ED 321 693)

Friedel, J.N., Coker, D.R., & Blong, J.T. (1991). *A survey of environmental scanning in U.S. technical and community colleges.* Paper presented at the annual forum of the Association for Institutional Research, San Francisco. (ERIC Document Reproduction Service No. ED 333 923)

Meixell, J.M. (1990) *Environmental scanning activities at public research and doctorate-granting universities.* Paper presented at the annual meeting of the Society for College and University Planning. (ERIC Document Reproduction Service No. ED 323 857)

committee is directed by the planning and budget office and consists of experts and community representatives.

Pritchett found common patterns in how the environmental scanning activity developed in these institutions. New presidential leadership and active governing boards were critical in two institutions; reductions in state appropriations and enrollment declines were influential at all three. In all institutions, presidential recognition and support for the formal scanning process were essential elements of the planning process.

GETTING STARTED

The first step in establishing environmental scanning is to decide which level of scanning commitment is best for your institution at this time: irregular, periodic, or continuous. Most colleges and universities operate an irregular or periodic system, focusing on the task environment. These levels require less resource commitment from the institution, but they only address the immediate needs for information about the external environment. You may satisfy the requirements of these levels through several means. A quick way of getting started is to interview major decisionmakers regarding their view of the most critical trends and developments that could affect the institution. Use the interviews and conversations with your colleagues (including those at other institutions) to identify

critical trends and potential developments. Also examine past program reviews, the last institutional self-study, and the most current master plan.

Establishing a continuous scanning system requires more effort and resources. First, secure a resource commitment from the senior official responsible for planning. At a minimum, a continuous scanning system requires a professional and a support person to devote half of their time to the enterprise. Further, a continuous scanning program requires a number of scanners who agree to rigorously and systematically review specific information resources. Assuming that you secure the resources, your next step is to recruit and train volunteers to perform active scanning.

Training

One approach to recruiting scanners is to offer a half- to full-day environmental scanning workshop. Invite faculty members from all disciplines as well as key administrators from all functional areas. Be sure to include members of the institution's planning committee as well as senior executives and members of the board of trustees and/or board of visitors, if appropriate. Heterogeneity of backgrounds, experiences, and perspectives guards against parochial viewpoints and will help you see into the future with less hindrance from the "blinders" of the past.

The invitation should convey the idea that environmental scanning information is essential for the institution and its academic departments. Also stress that the information obtained in the environmental scanning process will inform the ongoing strategic planning process. Participants are scanning for information that impacts the future of the institution and its programs.

After explaining how environmental scanning fits into external analysis and how external analysis is merged with internal analysis to formulate strategic plans (see **Figure 1**), initiate a series of exercises where participants identify and prioritize critical trends and emerging issues. These exercises allow participants to bring their individual knowledge of the external environment to the discussion and to develop an event and trend set to guide monitoring. Instruct participants to:

- *Seek signs of change.* Review the STEEP sectors, looking for signs of change. This requires examining sources for movement in relevant variables. For example, changes in the average SAT score of entering college freshmen or percentage of Black males applying for college could be significant to your institution.

- *Look for signals of potential events on the horizon.* For example, research on Alzheimer's disease may produce a drug with side effects to enhance memory capabilities. New research on solar or wind energy may portend significant savings in energy

costs. An increasing number of interactive videodiscs and CD Roms may signal a major change in how information is presented to students. All of these trends could have significant impact on higher education, with implications for faculty development programs.

- *Look for forecasts of experts.* Some experts maintain we are moving toward a sustainable world in which attention will focus on energy efficiency, recycling, protection of biological and environmental bases, and the feeding and stabilization of the world population. Ask participants to consider the implications of the experts' forecasts for your institution.

- *Look for indirect effects.* It is important to remember that many trends or events that do not have direct implications for your institution may have second- or third-order effects.

- *Be aware that there are few guidelines on how to do scanning.* There are no hard and fast rules that lead to "correct" interpretations. The data do not speak for themselves. Scanners' skills, abilities, experiences, and judgments are critical to interpreting the data.

- *Write abstracts.* Abstracts are excellent vehicles to crystallize thoughts and communicate what is known about changing trends and patterns. When preparing abstracts, write the lead sentence in response to these questions: "If I had only a few minutes to describe this trend to a friend, what would I say? What is the most important idea or event that indicates change?" The responses to these questions should be contained in a one-paragraph explanation. Whenever possible, include statistical data. Limit the summary to no more than one-half page of single-spaced, typewritten copy. Depending upon your institution's culture, you may want to include a statement of the implications of the article for the institution.

Monitoring Taxonomy

The trends and events identified in the initial workshop are the beginnings of a scanning/monitoring taxonomy. A scanning/monitoring taxonomy has two objectives: (1) to provide a comprehensive set of categories to organize information and (2) to provide a numbering method for storing information. The STEEP sectors are an elementary taxonomy. Each category is usually subdivided. For example, the social sector may be divided into education, values, and demographics. With an electronic bibliographic database program, it is easy to build your taxonomy "as you go," using keywords to denote the categories. Be aware that developing, storing, and maintaining an environmental scanning database requires a good deal of time and effort.

Scanning Resources

Overviews

Future Survey Annual and *Future Survey*. World Future Society, 4916 St. Elmo Ave., Bethesda, MD 20814. Phone: 301/656-8274.

John Naisbitt's Trend Letter. Global Network, 1101 30th St., NW, Ste. 301, Washington, DC 20007. Phone: 202/337-5960.

Marien, M. (1991). Scanning: An imperfect activity in an era of fragmentation and uncertainty. *Futures Research Quarterly, 7*(3), 82-90.

What Lies Ahead. United Way of America, 701 N. Fairfax St., Alexandria, VA 22314. Phone: 703/836-7100.

What's Happening. Wilkinson Group, 8128 Pine Lake Ct., Alexandria, VA 22309. Phone: 703/780-6170.

General Periodicals

Newspapers

The New York Times, 229 W. 43rd St., New York, NY 10036. Phone: 1-800-631-2500.

The Washington Post, 1150 15th St., NW, Washington, DC 20071. Phone: 1-800-477-4679.

The Wall Street Journal, 200 Liberty St., New York, NY 10281. Phone: 1-800-841-8000, ext. 472.

The Miami Herald, 1 Herald Plaza, Miami, FL 33132-1693. Phone: 1-800-825-MAIL.

Chicago Tribune, Tribune Tower, 435 N. Michigan Ave., Chicago, IL 60611. Phone: 1-800-TRIBUNE.

The Los Angeles Times, The Times Mirror Company, Times Mirror Square, Los Angeles, CA 90053. Phone: 1-800-LATIMES.

The Christian Science Monitor, The Christian Science Publishing Society, One Norway St., Boston, MA 02115. Phone: 1-800-456-2220.

The Times (of London), 1 Pennington St., London E19XN, England. Phone: 071-782-5000.

Magazines

Vital Speeches of the Day. See *Readers' Guide*.

Across the Board, Conference Board, Inc., 845 Third Ave., New York, NY 10022. Phone: 212/759-0900.

Time. See *Readers' Guide*.

Newsweek. See *Readers' Guide*.

Scannning Resources
General Periodicals (cont.)

U.S. News and World Report. See Readers' Guide.

Futures, Butterworth-Heinemann Ltd., P.O. Box 63, Westbury House, Bury St., Guilford, Surrey GU25BH, England. Phone: 048-330-0966.

Forum for Applied Research and Public Policy, University of Tennessee, Energy, Environment, and Resources Center, Knoxville, TN 37966-0710. FAX: 615/974-1838.

Atlantic. See Readers' Guide.

The Nation. See Readers' Guide.

Ms. See Readers' Guide.

The Futurist. See Readers' Guide.

Social/Demographic
Periodicals

American Demographics, Box 68, Ithaca, NY 14851-0068. Phone: 607/273-6343.

Public Opinion Quarterly. American Association for Public Opinion Research, University of Chicago Press, Journals Division, 5720 S. Woodlawn Ave., Chicago, IL 60637. Phone: 312/753-3347.

U.S. Government Agencies

U.S. Department of Commerce, National Technical and Information Services. See *GPO Monthly Catalog.*

U.S. Department of Labor. See *GPO Monthly Catalog.*

U.S. Department of Health and Human Services, National Center for Health Statistics. See *GPO Monthly Catalog.*

Associations

United States League of Savings Institutions, 1709 New York Ave., NW, Ste. 801, Washington, DC 20006. Phone: 202/637-8900.

American Council of Life Insurance, Social Research Services, 1001 Pennsylvania Ave., NW, Washington, DC 20004-2599. Phone: 202/624-2000.

International

United Nations, First Ave. & 46th St., New York, NY 10017. Phone: 212/963-1234.

Organization for Economic Cooperation and Development, 2, rue Andre Pascal, 75775, Paris Cedex 16, France. Phone: 1-45-24-8200.

Scanning Structure

The structure of the scanning system does not need to be elaborate. The chair of the scanning committee is responsible for assigning information sources to each scanner and for collecting and filing copies of articles and scanning abstracts. Assigning scanners specific materials for regular monitoring provides a measure of confidence that most "blips" on the radar screen will be spotted. In making this assignment, ascertain first what sources are reviewed regularly by the scanners. This list should be compared to the list of important information resources identified by the scanning committee. Assign scanners material they already regularly review. Also ask for volunteers to review material not regularly read by committee members. If there is an abundance of scanners, build in redundancy by having two or more scanners review the same information resource.

Periodically the planning committee should meet to sort, sift, and evaluate the significance of the abstracts the scanners write. At the conclusion, the planners should summarize by sector (i.e., social, technological, economic, environmental, and political) all abstracts for use in the institution's strategic planning process.

RESOURCES

There is no lack of resources available for environmental scanning. The 1988-89 *Future Survey Annual* lists 454 futures-relevant periodicals. Marien (1991) reports there are 46 publications in international economics and development, 45 in environment/resources/energy, and 31 in health and human services that frequently have futures-relevant information.

In addition, there are a number of general newspapers and magazines that each provide discussion on a broad spectrum of issues. Newspapers you should systematically scan include *The New York Times, The Washington Post, The Wall Street Journal, The Miami Herald, The Chicago Tribune, The Los Angeles Times, The Christian Science Monitor,* and *The Times* of London. Magazines include *Vital Speeches of the Day, Across the Board, Time, Newsweek, U.S. News and World Report, Futures, The Forum for Applied Research and Public Policy, World Monitor, Atlantic, The Nation, Ms,* and *The Futurist.*

The most important criterion for literature selection is diversity. To ensure that you adequately scan the task environment, industry environment, and macroenvironment, identify information resources in each of the STEEP sectors. If your institution does not have the human resources to implement a continuous scanning system, you may wish to employ a scanning service. Both Weiner, Erich and Brown, Inc. and the Wilkinson Group offer such services.

The Macroenvironment

In conjunction with its Program in Educational Leadership, the

Social/Demographic (cont.)

The UNESCO Future Scan: A Bibliographic Bulletin of Future-Oriented Literature. United Nations Educational, Scientific, and Cultural Organization, Place de Fontenoy, 75700 Paris, France. Phone: 1-45-68-1000.

Technological

Periodicals

Technology Review, Building W59, Massachusetts Institute of Technology, Cambridge, MA 02139. Phone: 617/253-8250.

Datamation. Cahners Publishing Company, Division of Reed Publishing Inc., 275 Washington St., Newton, MA 02158-1630. Phone: 617/964-3030.

Byte. See *Readers' Guide.*
Computer World. See *Readers' Guide.*
Discover. See *Readers' Guide.*
Infoworld. Infoworld Publishing, 1060 Marsh Road, Menlo Park, CA 94025. Phone: 415/328-4602.
Science. See *Readers' Guide.*
Scientific American. See *Reader's Guide.*
The Whole Earth Review. Point Foundation, 27 Gate Five Rd., Sausalito, CA 94965. Phone: 415/332-1716.

Associations

Proceedings of the National Academy of Sciences. National Academy of Sciences, Office of News and Public Information, 2102 Constitution Ave., NW, Washington, DC 20418. Phone: 202/334-2138.

Economic

Periodicals

Business Week. See *Readers' Guide.*
The Economist. Economist Newspaper, 10 Rockefeller Plaza, 10th Floor, New York, NY 10020. Phone: 212/541-5930.
Fortune. See *Readers' Guide.*
Money, Inc. See *Readers' Guide.*
The Monthly Labor Review. See *Readers' Guide.*

U.S. Government Agencies

U.S. Department of Commerce, Bureau of Economic Analysis. See *GPO Monthly Catalog.*
U.S. Department of Labor. See *GPO Monthly Catalog.*
U.S. Department of Energy. See *GPO Monthly Catalog.*

Scanning Resources
Economic (cont.)

U.S. Department of the Treasury. See *GPO Monthly Catalog.*

Environmental
Periodicals

Ecodecision. Royal Society of Canada, 276 Rue Saint-Jacque, Oest, Bureau 924, Montreal H24IN3 Canada.

Environment. Heldres Publications, 4000 Albemarle St., NW, Washington, DC 20016. Phone: 202/362-6445.

Associations

Global Tomorrow Coalition, 1325 6 St., NW, Ste. 915, Washington, DC 20005-3140. Phone: 202/628-4016

Worldwatch Institute, 1776 Massachusetts Ave., NW, Washington, DC 20036. Phone: 202/452-1999.

Island Press, 1718 Connecticut Ave., NW, Ste. 300, Washington, DC 20009. Phone: 202/232-7933.

Audubon Society, 950 Third Ave., New York, NY 10022. Phone: 212/832-3200.

Sierra Club, 730 Polk St., San Francisco, CA 94109. Phone: 415/776-2211.

Political
Periodicals

New Republic. See *Readers' Guide.*

The National Review. See *Readers' Guide.*

The National Journal, 1730 M St. NW, Ste. 1100, Washington, DC. Phone: 202/857-1400.

In These Times. Institute for Public Affairs, 2040 N. Milwaukee Ave., 2nd Fl., Chicago, IL 60647-4002. Phone: 312/472-5700.

Kiplinger Washington Letter. Kiplinger Washington Editors, Inc., 1729 H St. NW, Washington, DC 20006. Phone: 202/887-6400.

Mother Jones. See *Readers' Guide.*

Federal Register. U.S. Office of the Federal Register, National Archives and Records Administration, Washington, DC 20408. Phone: 202/523-5240.

Congressional Quarterly Weekly Report. Congressional Quarterly, Inc., 1414 22nd St., NW, Washington, DC 20037. Phone: 800-432-2250.

Institutes

Hudson Institute, Herman Kahn Center, 5395 Emerson Way, P.O. Box 26-919, Indianapolis, IN 46226. Phone: 317/545-1000.

University of North Carolina at Chapel Hill publishes *On the Horizon,* the environmental scanning newsletter for higher education. A comprehensive list of information resources by STEEP sector in the macroenvironment includes the following:

- *Social/demographic/values/ lifestyles.* Data from periodic publications or statistics from the Census Bureau and other federal, state, and local governmental agencies provide the basics on population trends and characteristics. The Department of Labor and the Department of Commerce's National Technical and Information Services make available specific types of demographic analyses. The National Center for Health Statistics provides data on trends in areas such as fertility and life expectancy. The U.S. League of Savings Associations studies changes in homebuyer demographics, and the American Council of Life Insurance's Social Research Services conducts demographic studies. The United Nations and the Organization for Economic Cooperation and Development publish periodic reports detailing international developments in this area.

- *Technology literature.* Discussion of technological advances and future possibilities can be found in a variety of periodic sources, including *Technology Review, Datamation, BYTE, Computer World, Discover, Infoworld, Science, Scientific American, The*

Scanning Resources
Political (cont.)

Institute for the Future, 2740 Sand Hill Rd., Menlo Park, CA 94025. Phone: 415/854-6322.

Brookings Institute, 1775 Massachusetts Ave., NW, Washington, DC 20036. Phone: 202/797-6000.

American Enterprise Institute for Public Policy Research, 1150 17th St., NW, Washington, DC 20036. Phone: 202/862-5800.

Associations

State Legislatures. National Conference of State Legislatures, Marketing Department, 1560 Broadway, Ste. 700, Denver, CO 80202. Phone: 303/623-7800.

• *Political literature*. What is happening in the political/legislative arena is covered by *New Republic, The National Review, The National Journal, In These Times, Mother Jones, Federal Register, and Congressional Quarterly Weekly Report*. Other sources include public opinion leaders, social critics, futures-oriented research institutes (e.g., the Hudson Institute and the Institute for the Future), public policy

Whole Earth Review, and *Proceedings of the National Academy of Sciences*.

• *Economic literature*. There are a number of periodicals focusing on economic trends and forecasts, including *Business Week, The Economist, Fortune, The Monthly Labor Review*, and *Money, Inc*. You can obtain monthly reports from the Department of Commerce's Bureau of Economic Analysis as well as reports from the Departments of Commerce, Labor, Energy, and Treasury. State and local governmental agencies provide regional economic data.

• *Environmental literature*. Recommended periodicals on the environment are *Ecodecision* and *Environment*. Several organizations publish futures-oriented reports on the environment (e.g., Global Tomorrow Coalition, Worldwatch Institute, and Island Press). The Audubon Society and Sierra Club also publish periodic reports in this area.

For scanning resources on higher education, see:

Periodicals

The Chronicle of Higher Education, 1255 23rd St., NW, Ste. 700, Washington, DC 20037. Phone: 202/466-1000.

Education Week. Editorial Projects in Education, Inc., 4301 Connecticut Ave., NW, Ste. 250, Washington, DC 20008. Phone: 202/364-4114.

Higher Education Daily. Capitol Publishers, Inc., 1101 King St., Ste. 444, Alexandria, VA 22314. Phone: 703/683-4100.

Newsletters

On the Horizon. Program in Educational Leadership, School of Education, University of North Carolina, CB3500 Peabody Hall, Chapel Hill, NC 27599. Phone: 919/966-1354.

Higher Education and National Affairs. American Council on Education, Publications Division, One DuPont Circle, Washington, DC 20036. Phone: 202/939-9450

Communication Network News. State Higher Education Executive Officers/National Center for Education Statistics, 707 17th St., Ste. 32700, Denver, CO 80202-3427. Phone: 303/399-3685.

Memo to the President. American Association of State Colleges and Universities, One DuPont Circle, Washington, DC 20036. Phone: 202/293-7070.

E-Mail

E-Mail News, Society for College and University Planning, Joanne Cate (Ed.), BUDLAO@UCCVMA.BITNET. Phone: 510/987-0963.

The Electronic AIR, Association for Institutional Research, Larry Nelson (Ed.), NELSON_L@PLU.BITNET.

College/University Scans

Cantonsville (Maryland) Community College. (1989). *External scan and forecast, 1989.* (ERIC Document Reproduction Service No. ED 309 817)

Osborn, F. (1989, May). *Environmental scan: A strategic planning document.* Rochester, NY: Monroe Community College. (ERIC Document Reproduction Service No. ED 307009)

Friedel, J. (1989, September). *2020 perfect vision for the next century: An environmental scan.* Bettendorf, IA: Eastern Iowa Community College District. (ERIC Document Reproduction Service No. ED 319 451)

Scanning Services

Weiner, Erich & Brown, Inc., 200 E. 33rd St., Ste. 9-I, New York, NY 10016. Phone: 212/889-7007.

Wilkinson Group, 8128 Pine Lake Court, Alexandria, VA 22309. Phone: 703/780-6170.

research centers (e.g., the Brookings Institute and the American Enterprise Institute for Public Policy Research), governmental documents, proposed bills to the legislature, and statements or opinions by social critics, experts, and activists. Finally, consult *State Legislatures* for a periodic summary of pertinent legislation being considered in state legislatures throughout the country.

• *Electronic databases.* There are a number of electronic databases containing up-to-date descriptions of articles (by title and, many times, by abstract) available on a subscription basis. ABI Inform, ERIC, and PAIS are a few examples. Two database services, Dialog and BRS, contain hundreds more databases spe-

cializing in all areas. Undoubtedly, your library already subscribes to these databases and database services. These resources are amenable to monitoring (i.e., to retrieving information about critical trends and potential events that you identified in your scanning). In addition, you can use electronic bibliographic databases to file and store information. Such programs facilitate review, referral, and updating. It is also possible to develop consortium relationships with other institutions by using an electronic filing system.

The Industry Environment

Key sources on the higher education industry environment include *The Chronicle of Higher Education, Education Week,* and *Higher Education Daily.* A number of newsletters serving the industry environment are available as well. In addition, many individuals and colleges/universities put their environmental scans on ERIC.

The following newsletter editors agree to respond to your questions if you are thinking of developing a newsletter for your campus:

Donna McGinty, Center for Continuing Education, University of Georgia, Athens, GA 30602. Phone: 404/542-3451.

Lowell Lueck, Director of Institutional Research and Planning, Western Illinois University, 312 Sherman Hall, Macomb, IL 61455. Phone: 309/298-1185.

Robert Wilkinson, Director of Institutional Research, 212 Russ Hall, Pittsburgh State University, Pittsburgh, KS. Phone: 316/231-7000.

Perhaps the most useful resource is your own network of friends and colleagues within the profession. Frequently you can phone a colleague at another institution and get information quickly. Or you can post your question in the Association for Institutional Research's or the Society for College and University Planning's electronic newsletters.

The Task Environment

Information resources for scanning the task environment include local, state, and regional newspapers, local and state government reports, and experts in demography, sociology, and political science departments in your institution.

COMMUNICATION

A scanning newsletter brings important trends and events to the attention of all members of your institution and, at the same time, provides recognition for the efforts of the scanners. Make the newsletter a "stand alone" document and distribute it widely. You may want to consider a logo, present the newsletter on distinctive paper, and have special boxes labeled "Wild Speculations," "Left Field," or "Wild Cards." The important point is that the newsletter only contain items that have implications for the institution. Solicit comments and contributions from all who read the newsletter, and make the format easy to read in form and content. An excellent vehicle for communicating the results of the scanning/monitoring committee's work is to distribute selected abstracts, drawing attention to the implications of a particular trend or potential event or series of inter-related trends and events.

REMEMBER

We all do informal environmental scanning. However, continuous scanning is required if decisionmakers are to understand, anticipate, and respond to the threats and opportunities posed by changes in the external environment. It is important that campus decisionmakers participate in this process. Through participation, they develop a shared understanding of high priority issues and a view of the dynamics of the changing environment.

Remember that environmental scanning is something of an art form; guidelines on how to scan are necessarily few. There are no hard and fast rules to lead to a "correct" interpretation of information. Be careful to structure your scanning process to minimize the possibility of being "blind-sided" by a change in the environment that you should have seen coming.

Finally, remember that environmental scanning is only one component of external analysis. It is the starting point, however, from which you and your colleagues can identify trends and events in the environment worthy of monitoring. More importantly, it provides a basis for discerning the strategic direction of your institution from which you may plan far more effectively.

Total Quality Management

Mary Ann Heverly

ISSUES

The management philosophy known as Total Quality Management (TQM) has captured the attention of American business and now higher education. A cardinal rule of TQM is that managerial actions and decisions should be guided by **data**. Actions and decisions without data only increase variation in the process and degrade its performance. In the absence of data, the Total Quality manager does **nothing** to fix or improve a process.

Supporting new TQM efforts on your campus requires that you become conversant with TQM philosophy, applications, and methods. To help you, this chapter addresses five basic questions:

- What is TQM and what are its origins?

- What are the TQM concepts?

- What does TQM have to offer higher education?

- What are TQM methods?

- What are the benefits and drawbacks of using TQM?

Mary Ann Heverly is the director of Institutional Research at Delaware County Community College, Media, PA. She is a member of the Publications Board of AIR.

ORIGINS

Many of the companies using TQM to achieve and maintain a competitive edge are Japanese. As a result, people often mistakenly assume that the method originated with the Japanese. Actually, TQM was the work of American and British statisticians who developed the statistical quality control concepts and methods used to support the Allied effort during World War II. Following WWII, American statisticians and quality experts, such as W. Edwards Deming and Joseph Juran, taught the methods to the Japanese. After this, statistical quality control evolved from a narrow specialty for engineers, statisticians, and "QC" practitioners into a philosophy of management that permeates the entire organization.

For the basic TQM concepts and history, see:

Ishikawa, K. (1985). *What is Total Quality Control?* (Lu, D.J.,Trans.). Englewood Cliffs, NJ: Prentice Hall.

Deming, W.E. (1986). *Out of the crisis.* Cambridge, MA: Massachusetts Institute of Technology.

Imai, M. (1986). *Kaizen: The key to Japan's competitive success.* New York: Random House.

Brassard, M. (1989). *The Memory Jogger Plus.* GOAL/QPC, 13 Branch St., Methuen, MA 01844. Phone: 508/683-3900.

Figure 1	
TQM Philosophy	**Traditional Philosophy**
Study the process	**Study the outputs**
Continuous improvement	Leave well enough alone
Prevention	Detection
Customer input	**No direct customer input**
Manager as coach	**Manager as authority figure**
Understand variation	Quick fix
Data driven	Opinion driven

The TQM odyssey has come full circle. In the 1980s, American industry became interested in TQM. Customers' heightened standards for quality filtered into the service sector and private and public organizations. Federal Express, recently awarded a Malcolm Baldridge Quality Award, served as a model for TQM application in the service sector. Federal Express recognized that its "product" was not a tangible object that can be fixed, reworked, or recalled for defects. Instead, service transaction was the heart of Federal Express' business. The importance of employee involvement, training, and education was heightened because the work of the organization was conducted through service transactions.

TQM returned to its origins when the United States military, four decades after using statistical quality control during World War II, adopted TQM practices to accomplish the efforts supporting Desert Storm. The Air Force Logistics Command and Military Airlift Command borrowed the Federal Express model and adapted it to the war effort, titling it "Desert Express."

CONCEPTS

A common theme among TQM writers is that application of TQM requires a major shift in the values and management approach of the organization and everyone in it. This shift requires a movement away from what TQM writers refer to as the **traditional management approach**. **Figure 1** illustrates this comparison.

In the TQM approach, *quality* is the central value and goal. Instead of compartmentalizing responsibility for quality to a special unit or a certain management level, TQM assigns responsibility for quality to each employee and empowers employees at all levels to identify and fix process problems. This focus on quality and empowerment impacts *processes* of the organization, the way the organization views *customers*, and the role of *managers*. Masaaki Imai's (1986) *Kaizen: The Key to Japan's Competitive Success* is a good

101

place to start in assimilating the many aspects of TQM into a coherent picture.

Process

Authors and advocates stress that TQM requires an organization to shift its focus from outputs to processes. At the heart of TQM is the concept of **continuous process improvement.** In the TQM approach, employees study processes continuously to assess how well they operate and to identify areas needing improvement. Improvements then are standardized to "hold the gains." To provide support for this continuous assessment, data gathering is ongoing. The objective is to promote the *prevention* of defects or mistakes in the product.

In contrast, TQM writers portray the traditional management approach as resistant to change, with a tendency to do things the "way we've always done them." The goals and supporting value structure of the traditional management approach center around outputs and hierarchy. Quality control (QC) relies on *inspection* of the product or service to detect defects or poor quality at the conclusion of the process. In this approach, responsibility for quality often is assigned to a QC unit or a certain level in the management hierarchy.

Customer

In the TQM approach, quality is measured in terms of the *customer*. Further, the ultimate aim of TQM is to go beyond customer *satisfaction* to customer *delight*, beyond *assessing* customers' current *de-* *mands* to *anticipating their future needs.*

TQM's use of the customer as the measure of performance and quality translates into an expanded definition of "customer." In the TQM approach, customers include not only *external* users of products and services but also *internal* customers, including staff within the organization. In a college or university, external customers could include students, parents, business, industry, government, and the community. Students, for example, are external customers of the computing center, registration system, and financial aid office. At the same time, institutional researchers are internal customers of these same operations, using the computer center's data files as the critical components in institutional research analyses.

As a result of this focus on customers, TQM organizations actively and systematically seek the input of both external and internal customers. This systematic approach is marked by continually tapping and probing customers, asking for their reactions and perceptions, and observing how they access and use the organization's products and services. This means that if your college or university were using the TQM approach, computing services would be asking you for input, investigating problems with the files and processes, and perhaps even involving you directly in process improvement. It also would mean, however, that your office would design and implement processes to obtain continuous input processes from your "customers."

In organizations using the traditional management approach, attention paid to customer satisfaction and needs varies. At one extreme is the organization that does not consult its customers at all, assuming that the organization's managers know customers' needs and/or that the organization can create the need. At the other extreme is the organization that frequently gathers data on customers but not in the systematic and proactive fashion required in the TQM approach. Missing almost completely from the traditional management approach is an appreciation of internal customers and the continuous data-gathering efforts to assess their needs.

Manager's Role

TQM writers emphasize that the manager's role is to enable employees to accomplish their work. The manager does this by making available the resources employees need, including education and training in the use of quality improvement tools. The tools enable employees to gather data to assess and improve the processes they operate. When something goes wrong, the manager asks "What is wrong with the process?" The manager's problem-solving approach is to empower employees to identify the root cause, which when eliminated or changed, prevents the problem from recurring.

TQM at DCCC

The experience of Delaware County Community College (DCCC) illustrates TQM in a higher education organization. DCCC's president made the commitment to TQM in 1986. The first year was devoted to training and education of the executive group. This group developed a 10-year plan for implementing TQM at the college.

Teaching TQM. Beginning in 1987, the college developed non-credit TQM workshops and seminars for local business and industry. In recent years the college adapted these offerings for government and education because of their growing interest in TQM. A credit certificate program was launched in 1991, and the first completers will receive their certificates in 1992.

Administrative Applications. The implementation plan called for DCCC to model the use of TQM by applying it to administration of the college. At first, project teams were selected to work on a limited number of process improvement efforts. Teams included employees who operated the process as well as employees who were internal customers of the process. Team members included staff from different departments and levels. Training occurred in conjunction with team members' work on process improvement. More recently, the application of TQM has expanded to include all administrative units. The objective is to bring regular management activities into alignment with the strategic plan and mission of the college.

Academic Applications. The application of TQM to the academic side has taken several different forms. The TQM model was used by faculty who were involved in a recently completed self-study for accreditation. The plan is to expand

TQM into the teaching/learning process over the next three to five years. Workshops on TQM were given for interested faculty in 1991 and 1992. One division of the college (Math, Science, Engineering, and Technologies) will pilot the application of TQM to the teaching/learning process.

IR and TQM

The role of institutional research in DCCC's implementation of TQM is to support the data collection, analysis, and interpretation activities generated by TQM.

For more information on TQM at DCCC, contact Mary Ann Heverly, Delaware County Community College, Media, PA 19063.

TQM advocates portray the traditional manager as a wielder of power. When things go wrong, the traditional manager asks "Who is responsible?" Lacking the tools to understand the organization's systems, the traditional manager jumps to quick-fix solutions that are based on opinion, not on actual data from the process. Because the quick fix treats symptoms rather than root causes, it increases variation in a system, degrading its efficiency and adversely affecting its outputs.

TQM AND HIGHER EDUCATION

Higher education's interest in TQM is increasing dramatically. Colleges and universities are sending representatives to TQM training and bringing in consultants for on-campus discussion. Sessions on TQM at national conferences, such as AIR's annual forum, are packed. The literature on TQM in higher education reflects this growing interest and draws out new implications and applications for higher education organizations.

This high level of interest is not surprising. Writers and advocates frequently point out that TQM and higher education are a good match because TQM offers higher education:

- a methodology for improving quality,

- a good fit with the values of higher education, and

- support for emerging trends in higher education.

Quality

TQM's focus on quality and claims of increased productivity and lowered costs strike a responsive chord in college and university administrators dealing with a decline in funding and increasing constituency demands for accountability. Ellen Earle Chaffee, vice chancellor of academic affairs of the North Dakota University System and 1991-92 AIR president, sees quality improvement as a principal concern for the future of higher education and TQM as a key component in the solution. She frequently cites the link between quality and accountability as a primary reason for North Dakota's commitment to the TQM approach.

Approximately two dozen colleges and universities have enough experience with implementing TQM to provide insights on its impact on their institutions. A recent survey by

Seymour and Collett (Seymour, 1991) examined the impact of TQM at these institutions and found the benefits included increased efficiency and effectiveness. TQM improved efficiency in processes by eliminating unnecessary steps, errors, and redundancies. Most survey respondents also reported savings in staff time to complete processes. Examples of improved effectiveness included better cooperation across departments, improved morale, a more focused understanding of the organization's mission, and monetary savings.

Values

TQM values complement those of higher education. Three that are particularly central to the TQM approach and find their match in the higher education value structure are *shared responsibility/active learning*, support for *continuous/*

For more information on TQM's fit with higher education, see:

Chaffee, E.E. (1990). Quality: Key to the future. *American Journal of Pharmaceutical Education, 54,* 349-352.

Cornesky, R., McCool, S., Byrnes, L., & Weber, R. (1991) *Implementing Total Quality Management in Higher Education.* Madison, WI: Magna.

Marchese, T. (1991). TQM reaches the academy. *American Association for Higher Education Bulletin, 44*(3), 3-9.

Seymour, D.T. (1991). TQM on campus: What the pioneers are finding. *American Association for Higher Education Bulletin, 44*(3), 10-13.

Sherr, L.A., & Teeter, D.J. (Eds.) Total quality management in higher education. *New Directions for Institutional Research, 71.* San Francisco: Jossey-Bass.

---

lifelong learning, and the centrality of *data/the empirical method.*

Shared responsibility/active learning. Central to TQM philosophy is the concept of empowerment and shared responsibility. Employees at all levels are responsible for the improvement of processes and are empowered to identify and correct problems. This involvement requires all employees to be active and critical thinkers. The counterpart of shared responsibility in higher education is the value placed on active learning and cooperative learning.

Continuous/lifelong learning. Active involvement in process improvement requires employees to learn new skills and improve their critical thinking skills. Education and training, not limited to TQM topics, include skill building, career development, and personal growth. In this model, the role of management becomes one of facilitator of that ongoing learning process.

The higher education correlate is obvious. Lifelong learning and the development of critical thinking skills lie at the heart of the higher education value structure. TQM operationalizes those values in day-to-day management and in the lives of administrators, faculty, staff, and students.

Data/the empirical method. Data and data-driven decision-making are central to TQM's process evaluation and improvement. This emphasis on data complements the value higher education places on the empirical method. Learning how to pose a question; identifying

Sources on assessment and classroom research include:

Cross, K.P., & Angelo, T. (1988). *Classroom assessment techniques: A handbook for faculty.* National Center for Research to Improve Postsecondary Teaching and Learning, Ste. 2400, School of Education Bldg., University of Michigan, Ann Arbor, MI 48109-2748. Phone: 313/936-2748.

Ewell, P.T. (1991). Assessment and TQM: In search of convergence. In L.A. Sherr & D.J. Teeter (Eds.), *Total quality management in higher education. New Directions for Institutional Research, 71,* 39-52. San Francisco: Jossey-Bass.

the appropriate data to gather; collecting, analyzing, and interpreting data; and communicating findings to others are activities central to both the scientific method and the TQM approach.

Emerging Trends

TQM philosophy and methods also support the emerging trends of *assessment* and *classroom research.*

Assessment. TQM and assessment have a number of points in common. Increasingly, institutions in the forefront of the assessment movement focus on identifying areas for improvement rather than evaluating outcomes or programs as "good" or "bad." This approach is compatible with TQM's emphasis on continuous process improvement. In addition, leaders in the assessment movement emphasize the importance of gathering data at various points throughout students' experiences with a college or university, not solely at entry and exit. In TQM language, data are gathered not only on the "outputs" of educational processes but

also at various points in the operation of the "processes." This promotes understanding of how the process operates and facilitates working "upstream" to prevent problems from occurring. Further, the assessment movement advocates the involvement of faculty and staff in assessment processes rather than identification of a small group of staff with sole responsibility for assessment. Assessment works best when faculty and staff share responsibility for assessment practices, just as TQM requires the sharing of responsibility for process improvement.

Classroom research. Classroom research examines processes that operate within the classroom. The model assumes that faculty are in the best position to gather data on what works. This assumption is similar to TQM's tenet that the people who operate processes are the ones who should be gathering data on the efficiency and effectiveness of those processes.

Classroom research is conducted cooperatively with students. It values their voices and uses their feedback to continually improve processes within the classroom. TQM would describe this as "listening to the voice of the customer" and using the information to guide continuous process improvement.

Another distinctive feature of classroom research is its emphasis on gathering data periodically throughout the semester. This provides the faculty members with frequent and timely feedback that identifies improvements that will be responsive to the needs of students. In TQM this would be described as "focusing on prevention" rather than on inspection.

TQM TOOLS

TQM's continuous process improvement is guided by the **Plan-Do-Check-Act** (PDCA) cycle. PDCA is embedded in the philosophy and context of TQM and does not serve any function outside that context. TQM tools and methods then provide support for the PDCA cycle.

Plan-Do-Check-Act

The Plan-Do-Check-Act (PDCA) cycle guides the quality improvement effort. In the *Plan* phase, employees involved with the operation of a process pay special attention to problems arising in the flow of the process or in the process outputs. They then develop a plan for improving the process based on the data gath-

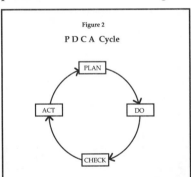

Figure 2

P D C A Cycle

ered. Implementation of the plan is termed the *Do* phase. During the *Check* phase, results of the improvement effort are assessed to determine their effectiveness. Events in the *Act* phase depend on the results. If no improvement oc-

curred, an alternate solution must be tried. If the results document improvement in the process, the newly implemented method is standardized to maintain gains in efficiency or effectiveness. See the Sherr and Teeter volume of *New Directions for Institutional Research* (1991) for illustrations of the use of the PDCA cycle in higher education.

Supporting the PDCA cycle are a set of basic tools used to characterize, study, and improve processes. Many are adaptations of tools and methods used outside TQM.

Flow Charts

Flow charts outline steps in a process. The *top-down flow chart* is the simplest, providing a starting point for understanding how a process should operate. The top-down

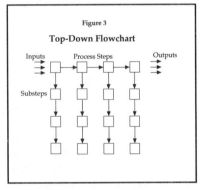

Figure 3

Top-Down Flowchart

Inputs   Process Steps   Outputs

Substeps

flow chart depicts the major steps in an ideal process. Complexities in the actual process (e.g., decision points, extra steps, rework) are not shown. The actual process can be depicted with a *process flow chart* outlining the activities that staff engage in to complete the process. Because the process chart shows complexities, decision points, feedbackloops, and extra steps, it helps identify areas for improvement. A *matrix flow chart* shows how the steps in a process flow over time and across departmental lines. The matrix flow chart is useful for identifying key members of a process improvement team. It also can help focus improvement efforts. For example, problems often occur at points where the process flows from one department to another. The matrix flow chart identifies these points.

Cause and Effect Diagram

The *cause and effect diagram* is also known as the *Ishikawa* or *fishbone diagram*. It uses a structured form of brainstorming to

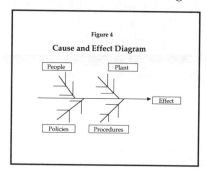

Figure 4

Cause and Effect Diagram

generate a list of proposed causes that contribute to an "effect," or problem. The effect, forming the head of the fishbone, is placed to the right of a horizontal axis, the backbone. Major categories form skeletal bones that radiate from the backbone of the diagram. In quality control, the categories are the four Ms: Manpower, Machines, Methods, and Materials. Categories better fitting administrative processes may include: People,

Plant, Policies, and Procedures. Causes are generated by brainstorming and are listed under the appropriate categories. The level of detail in the diagram indicates how successfully the activity has tapped team members' knowledge of the process.

The cause and effect diagram is useful for identifying the *most likely* causes of an effect. Data collection must follow to verify the major contributors to the effect under study.

Check Sheets

Check sheets facilitate data gathering and analysis. A check sheet might be developed to gather data on the potential causes identified by a cause and effect diagram. The critical characteristic

Figure 5		
Check Sheet		
Data Collector:		
Source of Data:		
Collection Dates:		
Category	Data	Sum
A	XXXXXX	6
B	XXXX	4
C	XX	2
D	X	1
E	X	1

of the check sheet is that it facilitates data collection. Data collectors are usually the persons who operate the process. An easy-to-use check sheet aids in gathering accurate data with minimal disruption of employees' daily work. Check

108

sheets also facilitate data analysis. A good check sheet aids in the quick computation of basic summary statistics, such as sums and

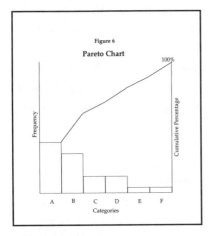

Figure 6

Pareto Chart

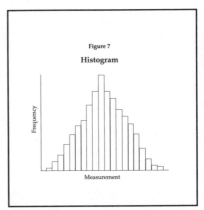

Figure 7

Histogram

ranges.

Pareto Chart

The Pareto chart displays data gathered on the frequency of problems and their potential causes. The Pareto chart is a bar graph that shows the categories represented by the bars in descending order, based on their frequency of occurrence. It often includes a second vertical axis that translates the frequencies into cumulative percentages. The Pareto chart identifies the *vital few* factors that account for the bulk of the problem. Teams use the Pareto chart to narrow the focus of their process improvement efforts by developing a process improvement plan that focuses on the vital few.

Histograms

The histogram displays the distribution of continuous (measurement) data. It conveys informa-

tion about the central tendency, variability, and shape of data gathered from a process. It reveals the nature of the process and can be used as a diagnostic tool.

Control Chart

The control chart is the principal statistical quality control tool. The purpose of the control chart is to determine whether a process is

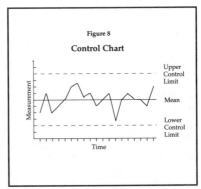

Figure 8

Control Chart

stable (contains only common cause variation) or unstable (contains special cause variation). Improvement efforts should be directed only toward stable processes. Unstable processes should be stabilized before attempting to improve them.

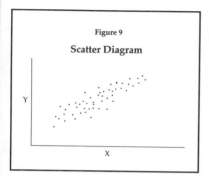

Figure 9

Scatter Diagram

Scatter Diagram

The scatter diagram displays the relationship between two variables. It is used when questions arise about possible cause and effect relationships between variables measured by continuous data. Although the scatter diagram cannot reveal whether one variable causes another, it can confirm or deny the existence of a relationship.

A Tool for Every Season

TQM is rich in methods and tools. It borrows tools from various disciplines and fuels the development of new tools. In addition to the basic tools used by persons at all levels of the organization, there are tools designed for specialized functions. For example, the *New Seven* Management Planning Tools (Brassard, 1989) and *Hoshin Planning* (King, 1989) aid in strategic planning.

For more on TQM tools, see:

Scholtes, P.R. (1988). *The team handbook: How to improve quality with teams.* Joiner Associates, P.O. Box 5445, Madison, WI 53705. Phone: 608/238-8134.

King, B. (1989). *Hoshin planning: The developmental approach.* GOAL/QPC, 13 Branch St., Methuen, MA 01844. Phone: 508/683-3900.

BENEFITS/ DRAWBACKS

Benefits

TQM offers much to colleges and universities seeking improved effectiveness, quality, and a sense of community. The benefits include:

- better use of resources,
- improved staff morale,
- increased cooperation across departments,
- better solutions to problems, and
- a heightened awareness of institutional mission.

Resources. Better use of resources results from studying processes. TQM stresses the identification and removal of unnecessary steps, rework, and error. This improved efficiency saves money, time, and other resources that can be directed toward value-added activities.

Morale. Improved morale among staff is an outgrowth of TQM's listening to the people who own and operate work processes. Employees appreciate having their voices heard and value improved, streamlined processes.

Cooperation. Cooperation across areas evolves in the TQM approach because processes cannot be improved unless all "owners and operators" of a process are working together. Since these owners and operators often work in different units, the improvement process cannot proceed until these staff are working together on the improvement effort.

Table 1	
Benefits and Drawbacks of TQM	
Benefits	**Drawbacks**
Better use of resources	Time and effort required
Improved morale	Resistance to culture change
Improved cooperation	Difficulty walking the talk
Better solutions	Unexpected events
Awareness of mission	

Solutions. TQM focuses attention on root causes rather than symptoms. Process improvement requires a basic understanding of PDCA and how to gather, analyze, and interpret data using the basic tools. This systematic approach leads to solutions that last because they are not quick fix solutions based on opinion or perception.

Mission. Finally, the TQM approach to planning sharpens employees' awareness of the institutional mission and priorities. Because strategic planning is tied to daily management activity in all units, staff become aware of how their work is tied to the work of the institution and to its future direction. The ultimate goal is an organization that has its departments internally aligned with strategic objectives.

Drawbacks

Reaping the benefits of TQM requires overcoming significant barriers to implementation, including:

- the time and effort TQM demands,
- resistance to changing the institution's culture,
- difficulties in "walking the talk," and
- impact of unpredictable "crisis" events.

Time and effort. TQM practitioners cite time and effort as a major drawback to implementation. It takes time to learn the tools, to learn about and assimilate the philosophy, and to change work methods. Once the employees and managers learn to use the tools and understand the philosophy, it takes time and effort to study processes and to collect and analyze data. TQM teams commonly report frustration stemming from the time required to gather data. Team members find

111

it hard to restrain themselves from jumping to solutions. Time also becomes a barrier when TQM is implemented in daily work. TQM can be viewed as an "add-on," and competing demands can leave staff feeling overwhelmed.

Culture. TQM requires change in the culture of most organizations. Resistance to change is strong and enduring. Because TQM requires years to implement across an institution and because it is an ongoing process that never ends, patience and fortitude are needed to accomplish the cultural transformation.

Walking the talk. Learning about TQM is easy when compared to the task of actually doing it—applying and modeling TQM. This barrier frustrates staff on two levels. First, it is difficult to translate the principles and apply the tools to daily work. Second, it is difficult even for strong proponents to consistently model TQM behavior. Reverting to former ways of managing is common, especially in times of stress.

Crises. Another barrier is the impact of unexpected or uncontrollable events. Examples include budget cuts, sudden demands from funding agents or governing bodies, and turnover of key staff who helped to drive the TQM implementation. Such events exacerbate the problems of time constraint and competing demands.

IR ROLE

As an institutional researcher, your expertise in data collection, analysis, and interpretation make you an integral part of TQM implementation, process improvement, and strategic planning. Because the PDCA cycle pushes staff to *use* the data they gather, a long-term result of TQM should be increased use of other institutional data, including data generated by IR studies.

Academic Program Review

Gary R. Hanson and Bridgett R. Price

ISSUES

Quality and effectiveness are terms that will dominate our thinking in higher education during the 1990s. While separate, these concepts also are interrelated. They share the same intended goal of helping the institution better achieve its mission. In addition, the attention focused on these concepts is driven by the same two forces: the **external** demand for accountability and the **internal** drive for program improvement. The key process for achieving quality and effectiveness is **academic program review**.

One way to look at academic program review is in terms of G.L. Gardiner's (1989) performance improvement cycle. In this model, the institutional mission statement drives the development of goals and objectives for intended student inputs, intended educational processes, and intended outcomes. The *input-process-outcomes* stages are used to evaluate and provide feedback for the improvement cycle. This information is neces-

sary to modify the actual process and outcomes of the academic program. A quality academic program review may require that you conduct all three kinds of assessment.

This chapter outlines the steps necessary to design, implement, and communicate the results of a typical academic program review. We organize the information around four key areas: Issues, Data, Analysis, and Communication. In each section, we present key questions and suggest possible solutions and resources. We break

Key references in academic program review include:

Kells, H.R. (1983). *Self-study processes: A guide for postsecondary institutions.* New York: Macmillan.

Gardiner, G.L. (1989). *Planning an assessment.* G.L. Gardiner, Department of Biological Sciences, Rutgers-The State University of New Jersey, Newark, NJ 07102-3192.

Peterson, G., & Haywood, P. (1989). Model indicators of student learning in undergraduate biology. In C. Adelman (Ed.), *Signs and traces: Model indicators of college student learning in the disciplines,* 93-122. Washington, DC: U.S. Government Printing Office.

Barak, R.J., & Breier, B.E. (1990). *Successful program review: A practical guide to evaluating programs in academic settings.* San Francisco: Jossey-Bass.

Astin, A.W. (1991). *Assessment for excellence: The philosophy and practice of assessment and evaluation in higher education.* New York: American Council on Education, Macmillan.

Gary R. Hanson is the coordinator of research, Office of Admissions at the University of Texas in Austin.

Bridgett R. Price is assistant professor of Behavioral Sciences and Leadership at the United States Air Force Academy.

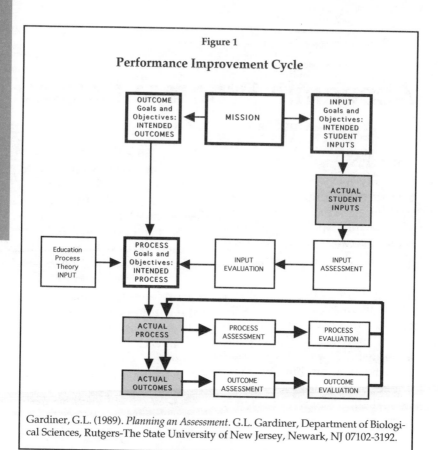

Figure 1

Performance Improvement Cycle

Gardiner, G.L. (1989). *Planning an Assessment*. G.L. Gardiner, Department of Biological Sciences, Rutgers-The State University of New Jersey, Newark, NJ 07102-3192.

this program review process into twelve steps, from identifying the problem through reporting the data. An example project is included in shaded boxes scattered throughout the chapter to illustrate a practical application.

Background

This chapter can only introduce you to the concept of academic program review and point to additional readings for more detailed information. If you have limited experience with program review, the resources listed in this chapter represent "background" reading. We highly recommend that these resources become part of your professional library and that you refer to them frequently.

Actual Project

Assume you are a member of a committee charged with conducting a self-study of the biology department. The biology department is expecting an accreditation site visit in approximately three years and the new accreditation standards demand evidence documenting outcomes and program review.

At first glance, the primary problem in conducting an academic program review is deciding *what* data to collect. However, academic program review is much more than that. Not only must you decide what data to collect, you must also consider your campus attitude toward program review.

Strategy

To begin a program review, you need to plan for how the project fits into the larger performance improvement cycle. You need to know *who* wants *what* kind of information from *whom*. Find out *why* the program review data are needed and *when* to collect the data. Although the steps outlined in this chapter appear to unfold in a linear fashion, the actual process is nonlinear because many of the elements are interrelated. A change in one element requires that you adapt other aspects of the plan.

STEP ONE. *Clarify expectations and develop an organizational strategy.*

Your first step is determining if what you are being asked to do is really program review. Refer again to Gardiner's (1989) performance improvement cycle. Where is your institution in the cycle? Have you been asked to examine only outcomes indicators, or do you also need data on student, faculty and staff characteristics, process, faculty workload, or research

Actual Project	
The committee clarifies its expectations of others and develops an organizational strategy. These questions will help you clarify what you should do. Assume that you and your committee have arrived at the following answers for your campus.	
Question	**On our campus . . .**
1. Why are we doing this project?	Accountability for an accreditation site visit
2. Who wants this program review done?	President and executive officers Regional accrediting agency Departmental chairs
3. When should the project be completed?	Six months before the accreditation site visit
4. What is the total time frame for the project?	Three years
5. Who will pay for the project?	Contingency funds from biology department to supplement IR office budget
6. Where is the administrative home?	IR office
7. Who should be involved in the planning?	Department faculty, selected advisory staff
8. Who are the local campus experts we can call on for help?	Testing center director, faculty in biology, psychology, sociology, and statistics departments.

productivity? Talk with individuals involved in the project and become familiar with their expectations.

If an academic program review is appropriate, determine whether the motivation behind the project is accountability or program improvement. If the purpose is accountability, focus on assessing what students have learned. If, on the other hand, the emphasis is on program improvement, link the assessment of outcomes to specific program components. Determine how and to what extent the program produces the outcomes. You need different kinds of evidence and data collection procedures depending on which purpose drives the study.

influence what you review, how you review it, and, most importantly, how you report the results. Think of ways to include as much of your campus community as possible.

STEP TWO. *Identify organizational barriers and limitations.*

If you have never conducted an academic program review before, be prepared to encounter a long list of barriers and limitations—reasons why the project shouldn't be started, conducted, or finished. Expect resistance to the concept of academic program review and know that your efforts may not be recognized or rewarded. The best way to handle these barriers is to identify them before you begin.

Actual Project

At this stage of the project, the committee identifies the lack of interest on the part of most of the biology department faculty and the intangible costs of overworking your own staff as two possible barriers to the project.

Second, a good organizational strategy requires that you ask who wants the data. Look beyond the obvious to the political realities within your campus community. You, your committee, the president, the department chair, and the accrediting agency may want the data, but there may be others not readily apparent with vested interests in the data. For example, other academic departments with upcoming accreditation site visits may scrutinize your review activities. Ask how they may benefit from this effort and build political bridges for your next program review effort. The interests of numerous constituent groups may

Astin (1991, see chapter 7) has an excellent list of academic games faculty and staff play to resist the assessment results.

STEP THREE. *Decide WHAT should be assessed.*

How will you know when the academic department is accomplishing its goals and objectives? What evidence is needed to document what students have learned and whether the process of delivering the academic programs is working well? Answering this question requires that you define the criteria by which the program will be evaluated. This single act may be your most frustrating experience; yet, understand that only extensive discussion within your campus community will produce a thorough and comprehensive program review. If this discussion doesn't happen, *stop the project until it does*. This is one step you cannot omit.

How do you foster that dialogue and debate? First, look to your institutional mission statement for clues. Then, look at specific departmental and service agency goals and objectives. Gardiner (1989) is an excellent resource for translating goals and objectives into assessable behaviors and attitudes. Look also at what others, such as Barak and Breier (1990), have done to find models, definitions, and project examples. More than likely, you will adapt what they have defined, but other projects provide a starting point for discussion.

One of the most difficult problems to overcome will be the tendency to review all aspects of the academic program. Barak and Breier suggest several categories of indicators representing important review criteria:

- program enrollments
- program completion rates
- faculty workload productivity
- program costs
- graduate outcomes
- labor market needs
- student satisfaction with course-work
- program autonomy

STEP FOUR. *Select an appropriate unit of analysis for your study.*

Indicators of an effective academic program review can be collected and analyzed at various levels. Before collecting data, determine the unit of analysis. Will you be looking at the results for individual students, or faculty, or a class or a group of students who participate in a specific program? Do you want to compare different types of evidence across several various class levels of students? Should all ranks of faculty be included? If you are unsure at this point, collect data at the lowest possible level and aggregate later.

STEP FIVE. *Decide WHO should be assessed and WHEN.*

Who should be included in the assessment depends on why you are conducting the study and what kinds of group comparisons you will make. If the purpose is accountability and you want to generalize the results across the entire department, you may want to collect evidence from a random sample of faculty and students. If, on the other hand, the purpose is to provide information to the biology department for the purpose of improving specific courses within the curriculum, collect data from a subset of biology courses. If the purpose is to document a change in the faculty workload over the past five years, you may need to collect data from institutional records for all faculty who generated credit hours of instruction within the department over that time period.

117

Actual Project

During the initial planning stage, discussion among the committee members focuses on what to measure and from whom the data should be collected. The committee reviews the institutional mission statement as well as the goals and objectives of the biology department. The committee decides to focus its efforts on student outcome evidence, program enrollments, and faculty workload indicators. It decides to collect evidence across three broad types of outcomes—general educational outcomes, discipline-specific outcomes, and selected noncognitive, or affective, outcomes. The committee decides to assess a random sample of all graduating seniors (for comparison purposes). Since the number of graduating seniors in the biology department is relatively small, the committee will collect outcomes assessment data from all graduating seniors in the department's majors. The committee finds the work on defining student outcomes for the biology discipline by Peterson and Hayward (1989) useful.

The outcomes assessment plan looks like this:

Sample	Type of Evidence
Program Enrollment	
All first-time majors who enrolled in the biology department over the last five years	Number of students enrolled
Faculty Productivity	
All full-time and part-time faculty, graduate teaching assistants, and instructors who taught courses in the biology department over the last five years	Total number of credit hours taught by level of instructional faculty

Sample	General Education	Type of Outcome Discipline-specific	Noncognitive
Graduating seniors (a random sample) and all graduating biology seniors	Critical thinking Writing skills Verbal/Oral		Civic responsibility Open-mindedness Moral development Intellectual integrity
All graduating biology seniors		Knowledge of biology (cognitive and lab skills)	Professional values and attitudes

Note: The taxonomy by Peterson and Hayward will be used to define key learning outcomes.

COLLECTING DATA

The goals of collecting data for your program review project can be accomplished using a variety of techniques. There are no right or wrong methods, merely choices that allow different results. The most obvious form of data collection is to find someone else on campus with the completed study you need. Yet, this strategy often is overlooked. On many occasions, the data or evidence will not be exactly what you want, but the results from a previous study may help answer your questions. If someone else has not conducted an applicable study, you need to make a series of important decisions about your data collection methodology. Follow these general guidelines.

STEP SIX. *Select data collection methods.*

Keep an open mind about the methodology for data collection. Be aware that different methodologies produce different answers; hence, the more techniques and methods you have at your disposal, the more likely you will choose just the right combination for a particular application. As a general rule of thumb, use multiple measures to assess each student outcome. Jean Endo's chapter in this *Primer* provides directions for conducting longitudinal student impact studies and developing questionnaires.

STEP SEVEN. *Identify outcomes indicators.*

Indicators can be direct or indirect. A direct indicator of a student's laboratory skill might be a videotape of the student conducting an experiment. An indirect indicator of values and attitudes toward the discipline might be inferred from the responses to a survey. At this stage, considerable discussion is required to achieve consensus about the outcome indicators that will be acceptable.

STEP EIGHT. *Identify "points of contact" for data collection.*

High levels of student, faculty, and administrative staff participation are required for effective academic program review. How do you "encourage" students, staff, and faculty to participate in the project? The best method is to identify those "points of contact" where you have a willing and captive audience. Each campus will have a different set of points of contact. Some of the more common points of contact with students are during admission or registration, on the first day of class, at the time of fee payment, at campuswide convocations or presentations by invited speakers, or when students submit required forms. Departmental meetings, mail, and planning retreats are possible points of contact with faculty. When points of contact do not exist or are not useful for a particular group, it may be necessary to create them. For example, you could create a "data collection" day when all students and faculty are required to participate in the collection of academic program review data instead of attending classes. You may need to call a special meeting of the college or department to draw faculty. However, recognize that mandatory participation may have an adverse impact on the data you collect.

STEP NINE. *Determine how many individuals to include in the process.*

How many students, faculty, and staff should you contact? While this question is often the first one asked, it should be one of the last answered because so many

Actual Project

During this stage of the academic program review, committee discussions take a long time. A great deal of debate occurs when the discussion begins to focus on the indicators that will be used to assess the proposed outcome dimensions or constructs. The table below shows the type of evidence, the assessment strategy used to collect the data, the indicators used as evidence, the estimated sample sizes, and the points of contact when the data would be collected.

Evidence	Assessment Strategy	Indicators	Sample Size	Point of Contact
Program Enrollment	Registrar's records	Number of students enrolled	all students	admission
Faculty Productivity	Office of Institutional Research	Number of credit hours	all courses in the biology department	semester census date
General Education Outcomes				
Critical thinking	Self-report	Scores on Glasser-Watson Test of Critical Thinking	a,b	Month before graduation
Writing skills	Self-report	Departmental writing exam	a,b	same
Oral presentation	Performance measure	Videotape of oral presentation of senior project	a,b	senior year
Noncognitive Outcomes				
Civic responsibility	Self-report	Checklist of student volunteer activities	a,b	Month before graduation
Open-mindedness	Self-report	Locally developed survey questions	a,b	same
Moral development	Inventory	Defining Issues Test	a,b	same
Intellectual integrity	Self-report	Locally developed survey questions	a,b	same
Discipline-specific Outcomes				
Knowledge of biology	Inventory	College Board Achievement Test	b	Month before graduation
Lab skills	Performance measure	Videotape of lab experiment	c	senior year
Professional values and attitudes	Self-report	Survey questions developed by biology faculty	b	Month before graduation

a A random sample of 100 non-biology graduating seniors

b All graduating biology majors (N = 115)

c A random sample of 25 biology graduating seniors

factors influence the decision. To determine how many individuals to include in your program review project, ask whether everyone should be assessed. If the answer is YES, you will know what to do. If the answer is NO, then you must decide how you want to limit the

Table 1

Guide to Handling Data

Type of Data	Data Capture	Data Storage	Data Retrieval
Qualitative	Paper files	Journals, logbooks, interview transcriptions, or notes	Manual, microcomputer, text file retrieval, hypermedia
	Video/audio recorder	Magnetic tape	Manual or hypermedia software retrieval
Quantitative	Paper files	Rating/scoring sheets	Manual
	Manual data entry via computer terminal	Magnetic disk or tape	Database software structured query language statistical analysis software
	Optical scan sheets	Magnetic disk or tape	Same
	Computer-assisted data collection	Magnetic disk or tape	Same

available pool of students. Consider the stability of your statistics within the smallest unit of analysis, the level of confidence or accuracy you want for the data, and the cost of collecting the data.

STEP TEN. *How do you capture and store data?*

Collecting, storing, and retrieving program review data requires a database. How you define and structure this database will determine the strength of your analysis and how easily you can generate useful reports. Crucial questions to ask before designing your database are:

- How will you convert individual participant responses to a safe and reliable storage system?

- Do you need to collect, store, and retrieve all possible data elements?

- Do you need to integrate your data with other student databases?

- How long will you keep the data "on-line?"

- Do you need to track the same cohort or sample of participants across multiple units of time?

- Do you need to track multiple samples in the same database?

- Do you need to keep individual participant records (i.e., one record per individual) or can you store aggregate or summary data?

- What medium will you use to store data? Paper files? Microcomputer? Mainframe database?

There are essentially three ways to collect data from students, faculty, and staff. First, you may collect data interactively by asking participants questions and using their responses to guide the next

121

question asked. Face-to-face or telephone interviews and interactive hypermedia computer software are ways to collect this kind of evidence. Second, you may gather self-reported data via a written questionnaire or examination. This is a broad category that covers standardized testing, computer-assisted data collection, and optical scan sheet coding. The data collection principle, however, is that the participant is required to "write" a response to your question. Third, you may observe participant behavior without direct interaction. **Table 1** shows how different types of data can be captured, stored, and subsequently retrieved.

Another important step in capturing and storing data is conducting a quality control check on the data you collect. To prevent "garbage" being stored in your program review database, you must make a few precautionary safeguards.

- *Conduct data audits* as you enter the data into your database. An "audit" is a quality control check of your data at the time the data are entered into your database. Most audit checks determine whether the data you enter fall within appropriate or "expected" ranges.

- *Conduct a data edit,* which involves "fixing the problem data" you find in the audit process. You will need a method to "recall" specific individual records, change a given data

element, and restore the "corrected" data record.

- *Pull a small random sample and proofread* the database version against the original version. The purpose for this check is to determine whether or not systematic data entry errors were made that may not show up in the audit process.

- *Compute simple frequency distributions* on all numeric data and list textual data. Finally, conduct an "eyeball" audit to make sure you have eliminated all the "garbage."

ANALYSIS

If you planned your academic program review well, analysis will be simple and straightforward. However, the data you collect are not always the data you anticipated. During the course of the project, a number of factors may intervene to influence the type or usefulness of the data. The purpose of the review may change during the weeks and months of data collection, the stakeholders may change, or the quality of data may fall short of initial expectations.

STEP ELEVEN. *Determine if the data are reliable.*

Review your data collection procedures and conduct preliminary statistical analyses to determine the quality of your data. If standardized scales and instruments were used, conduct reliability analyses. If your sample did not respond in an accurate and reliable manner, there is little use in continuing the analysis. Even if the instrument worked well on another college campus, it may not work well with your sample. Remember that reliability is not a property of the instrument but is a property of a given sample of participants responding to a particular instrument at a particular point in time. The reliability of an instrument used to assess a group of individuals need not be as high as an instrument used to make individual decisions (Astin, 1991). Scales comprised of three or four items may provide sufficient reliability for your program review.

In addition, check the range and completeness of the data. Did participants respond to all questions? Did they respond with answers that did not conform to your expectations? Did participants understand the directions and procedures for completing the instrument?

STEP TWELVE. *Select statistical techniques.*

There are basically three kinds of statistical analyses used to answer most program review questions:

- *Summary descriptive statistics* include simple numbers, frequency counts, percentages, and mean/median/mode statistics. For example, what percentage of the graduating seniors passed the collegewide writing examination?

- *Group comparisons* usually involve the comparison of one or more summary statistics, such as a mean or percentage across groups. For example, do full professors generate more instructional credit hours than do assistant professors?

- *Correlational techniques* are used to examine the nature and extent of the relationship between two or more variables in an outcomes study. For example, what is the relationship between the SAT Verbal test score and the four-year graduation rate? Although most correlational techniques do not allow you to make causal inferences, the use of path analysis does.

The statistics you use depend on the nature of your data (categorical, interval, or ratio), the assumptions you are willing to make about the size and shape of the data, and such practical considerations as the availability of statistical analysis software, computer time, and knowledgeable staff.

There are two important caveats about data analysis. First, do not use statistical techniques beyond the sophistication level of your audience. Second, do not try to use the same statistical technique to answer every research question. Rarely can all research questions be answered using one statistical technique.

COMMUNICATION

The usefulness of academic program review analysis depends ultimately on how the information is presented. It requires that the institutional researcher have perspective and flexibility.

Actual Project

Once the program review is in place, the responsibility for the data collection and analysis is turned over to the the the Office of Institutional Research. Locally developed instruments are pretested on small samples of students and revised. Commercial instruments are purchased and administered during the last month before graduation. The department faculty identified key classes that all seniors are taking and declared an "assessment" day for the data collection effort. Their cooperation also is instrumental in collecting videotape evidence for a small sample of students who are doing laboratory experiments and field work. Institutional database files for the enrollment and instructional credit hour production were obtained. The chart below summarizes the types of data collected and the analysis strategies used.

Variables	Data	Data Analysis	Summary Statistic
Program Enrollment Data	Headcount data by class	Descriptive Group comparison by class level	Ns and %s Means and t-tests
Faculty Productivity	Number of credit hours	Descriptive Group comparison by faculty level	Ns and %s Means and t-tests
General Education Outcomes			
Critical thinking	Scores on Glasser-Watson Test of Critical Thinking	Descriptive Group comparison	Mean and s.d. Means, t-test
Writing skills	Self-report	Descriptive Group comparison	Percent passing Test of proportions
Departmental writing exam	Graded exam score	Descriptive Group comparison	Percent passing Test of proportions
Oral presentation	Oral presentation of senior project	Descriptive Group comparison	Percent passing Test of proportions
Noncognitive Outcomes			
Civic responsibility	Checklist of student volunteer activities	Descriptive Group comparison	Percent checked Test of proportions
Open-mindedness	Locally developed survey items	Descriptive Group comparison	Percent checked Chi-square of item responses
Moral development	Defining Issues Test	Descriptive Group comparison	Percent each stage Mean total score Test of means
Intellectual integrity	Locally developed items	Descriptive Group comparison	Percent checked Chi-square of item responses
Discipline-specific Outcomes			
Knowledge of biology	College Board Achievement Test	Descriptive	Mean, s.d., and percent above a score of 600
Lab skills	Videotape of lab experiment	Descriptive	None
Professional values and attitudes	Locally developed items by biology faculty	Descriptive	Percent with Agree or Strongly Agree

One reason you need perspective and flexibility is that presentation is a highly dynamic point in the review process. Presentation of your findings is a step in a program improvement cycle. Your findings are not the end product of a closed model but form a major component in the critical feedback loop. You aren't finished. You have just begun.

Another reason you need perspective and flexibility is that this point in the program review process works best when it is participative. You are the facilitator in establishing opportunities for that participation. Your task is to involve (a) others in interpretation of the findings, (b) your audience in the implications of the data, and (c) your program review team in other campus issues.

Once you have compiled and summarized the evidence from the program review, involve others in making sense of the results. Do not attempt to interpret the evidence alone! Rather, involve individuals with as many diverse perspectives as possible. The greatest benefit of involving others is the shared "ownership" of the findings. These individuals play an important role in understanding the results. Let them do the work of communicating the findings.

Make the presentation of the results participative, too. Involve the audience in the presentation. Do not talk "to" the audience, rather present a little evidence and ask what they think it means. Ask what conclusions they draw from the data or what actions they believe should be taken. Most importantly, listen to what they say and then translate their suggestions into recommendations for action. Your program review is worthless if it does not contribute to program improvement or accountability.

Finally, academic program review results make no sense when interpreted in a vacuum. Your program review team must know and care about other campus issues. Understand the internal and external forces that shape your institution's mission and use that information to establish a context for understanding your academic program review results. Involvement in other campus issues not only helps you understand the relative importance of the academic review results but also provides another way to communicate the results. Other campus issues may benefit from what you have learned from the academic program review. Never lose a chance to share the results with whomever will listen.

> **For help in presenting results and recommendations, see:**
>
> Mims, R.S. (Ed.). (1987). *The design, production and use of computer graphics: A tutorial and resource guide.* Tallahassee, FL: Association for Institutional Research. (ERIC Document Reproduction Service ED 287 468)
>
> McLaughlin, J.A., Weber, L.J., Covert, R.W., & Ingle, R.B. (Eds.). (1988). Evaluation utilization. *New Directions for Program Evaluation, 39.* San Francisco: Jossey-Bass.
>
> Clagett, C.A. (1990). *Interpreting and presenting data to management.* (AIR Professional File No. 36.) Tallahassee, FL: Association for Institutional Research.

REMEMBER

Academic program review easily can get out of hand, become too large or ambiguous, and raise unconstructive hostility. To be effective, it is critical that the process be focused and directed. A clear understanding of the purpose—accountability or program improvement—is key. You must know who wants the data and why. Not all purposes are constructive or legitimate.

The central component to the process of program review is defining the criteria by which the program will be evaluated. Do not overlook or downplay this step.

At this point, a high degree of consensus is critical, and process is as important as product.

Your role in academic program review is to facilitate the process. Get involved early in order to shape the criteria used to evaluate the program. Stay late to make sure the findings are distributed throughout your campus. In between, work to establish the quality of the program review design, data collection, analysis, and interpretation. At the end, congratulate yourself for improving the academic program for faculty, staff, and students.

Cost Analysis

Heather J. Haberaecker

ISSUES

Colleges and universities use cost analysis to (1) justify requests for new positions, (2) support claims of accountability and increased productivity, and (3) resist cost reduction efforts. Presidents, vice presidents, and deans ask institutional researchers to compute the cost of an academic program or unit to support or discredit initiatives in these areas.

Brinkman (1988), in a review of higher education cost analyses, found cost analyses take several forms: (1) cost determination analysis, (2) explanatory cost analysis, and (3) evaluative cost analysis. **Cost determination analysis** classifies expenditures into discrete categories to determine the real cost. **Explanatory cost analysis** explains relationships between the determined cost and output (e.g., determining the cost per unit of output). **Evaluative cost analysis** includes elements of both cost determination and explanatory cost analyses to compare the costs of two or more units to determine their efficiency.

Heather J. Haberaecker is assistant vice president for budget and finance at Northeastern Illinois University, Chicago. She is 1992-94 treasurer for AIR.

Most cost analyses combine cost determination, explanation, and evaluation to answer these questions:

- How much does an activity cost per unit of output?
- How do our costs compare to others?

This chapter provides the tools to answer these questions. We use an example involving an academic department to illustrate the steps and decisions required in completing a cost analysis. The references and data sources provide a starting place for you to learn more about cost analysis.

BACKGROUND

The fundamental concepts in cost analysis were developed by cost accountants for private industry in the 1920s and 1930s. Procedural in nature, these practices were bolstered in the 1960s and 1970s by basic research to determine the factors that influence cost. However, until the merging of data processing with cost accounting, cost analysis was difficult to accomplish, particularly in large, complex higher education institutions. In the mid-1970s, the National Center for Higher Education Management Systems (NCHEMS) and the National Association of College and

These references contain discussions of cost analysis theory and application:

Lingenfelter, P.E. (1983). The uses and abuses of interstate comparisons of higher education funding. *Business Officer, 17*(3), 14-16.

Simpson, W.A. (1984). *Building an institutional costing model.* East Lansing, MI: Michigan State University. (ERIC Document Reproduction Service ED 252 150)

Taylor, B.J.R. (1986). *The calculation and presentation of management information from comparative budget analysis.* (AIR Professional File No. 24). Tallahassee, FL: Association for Institutional Research. (ERIC Document Reproduction Service ED 336 044)

Lane, F.S., Lawrence, J.S., & Mertins, H., Jr. (1987). University financial analysis using interinstitutional data. In P.T. Brinkman (Ed.), Conducting interinstitutional comparisons, *New Directions for Institutional Research, 53*, 83-101. San Francisco: Jossey-Bass.

Brinkman, P.T. (1988). *The cost of providing higher education: A conceptual overview.* State Higher Education Executive Offices., 707 Seventeenth St., Ste. 2700, Denver, CO 80202-3427. Phone: 303/299-3687.

University Business Officers (NACUBO) jointly developed detailed procedures for college and universities to use in determining cost. NCHEMS' and NACUBO's efforts were strengthened by the development of a Classification of Instructional Programs (CIP) taxonomy by the National Center for Education Statistics. This taxonomy enables higher education institutions to classify their instructional outputs so the outputs can be associated with the determined costs and compared to the costs at other institutions.

The literature of the 1980s reflects two trends: (1) a refinement of the theories underscoring the early procedural approaches to cost analysis, and (2) development of a new use of cost data—ratio analysis.

Refining Theory

Taylor (1986), Simpson (1984), and Brinkman (1988) are examples of discussions of theory and its refinement in application. Lingenfelter (1983) and Lane, Lawrence, and Mertins (1987) explored comparative cost analyses and identified many examples of inappropriate uses in higher education.

Ratio Analysis

Peat, Marwick, Mitchell & Company (1982) developed a new approach to using cost data called "ratio analysis." Rather than focusing on the cost, ratio analysis highlights the relationship between two categories of expenditures. For example, the ratio of

Sources on ratio analysis include:

Peat, Marwick, Mitchell, & Co. (1982). *Ratio analysis in higher education.* (Second edition). KPMG Peat Marwick, 3 Chestnut Ridge Rd., Montvale, NJ 07645. Phone: 201/307-7000.

Smith, T.Y. (1991). *Discipline cost indices and their applications.* Paper presented at the annual forum of the Association for Institutional Research, San Francisco. (ERIC Document Reproduction Service ED 336 044)

instruction to research is a ratio used to interpret an institution's relative balance between these areas. John Minter of the National Data Service for Higher Education pioneered a new area of consulting by making ratio data available to higher education institutions in a format supporting interinstitutional comparisons. Now Smith (1991) has taken the ratio concept to the discipline level.

DATA

Data supporting cost analysis is drawn from your institution's financial and academic systems. Data for interinstitutional comparisons comes from outside your institution.

Institutional Data

Cost analysis relates appropriate financial and course data to yield a cost per course. Your institution's financial accounting system and academic course files are the sources of these data. The financial accounting system contains budget and expenditure data by account. Within this system, account structure often mirrors the academic department organizational structure as well as identifies source of funds (e.g., state funds by account). Within an account, object codes identify specific types of expenditures (e.g., faculty salaries). By using account and object code, you can extract the financial data at the level needed in a cost analysis.

The academic course files of most institutions contain student registrations by course. Course numbering systems identify the course's academic level. Using CIP codes, you can organize course data by discipline. This organization makes interinstitutional instructional comparisons possible. Relating the cost account structure to the course CIP structure makes it possible to compute a cost per unit of instruction (e.g., cost per SCH).

> **For procedures for determining cost in higher education, see:**
>
> National Center for Higher Education Management Systems, and National Association of College and University Business Officers. (1977). *Procedures for determining historical full costs: The costing component of NCHEMS information exchange procedures.* (Technical Report 65, second edition). Boulder, CO.
>
> National Center for Higher Education Management Systems. (1979). *Evaluation of IEP costing procedures: A pilot study by six major research universities.* Boulder, CO.
>
> **For the latest CIP code structure, see:**
>
> Morgan, R.L., Hunt, E.S., & Carpenter, J.M. (1991). *Classification of instructional programs, 1990 Ed.* National Center for Education Statistics, 555 New Jersey Ave., NW, Washington, DC 20208-1405. Phone: 202/357-6828.

Comparative Data

There are several sources of external cost data available for interinstitutional cost comparisons. The Integrated Postsecondary Education Data System (IPEDS) Finance Survey is the primary source of comprehensive financial data across all U.S. higher education institutions. You may obtain this data directly from the federal government through the Office of Educational Research and Improvement or through several vendors, including NCHEMS and John Minter. NCHEMS and most other vendors are willing to customize the data in a variety of formats and institutional datasets.

The following are sources of cost data:

Brinkman, P.T. (1985). *Instructional costs per student credit hour: Differences by level of instruction.* Boulder, CO: National Center for Higher Education Management Systems (ERIC Document Reproduction Service ED 270 063)

State of Illinois Board of Higher Education. (1991). *1989-90 Academic discipline unit cost study and 1989-90 comparative cost study for Illinois public universities.* 500 Reisch Bldg., 4 West Old Capitol Square, Springfield, IL 62701. Phone: 217/782-2551.

Office of Educational Research and Improvement
U.S. Department of Education
555 New Jersey Ave., NW
Washington, DC 20208-5725
Phone: 202/219-1847

National Center for Higher Education Management Systems
P.O. Drawer P
Boulder, CO 80301-9752
Phone: 303/497-0301

Grapevine
Center for Higher Education
Illinois State University
Normal, IL 61761-6901
Phone: 309/438-5405

The Chronicle of Higher Education
1255 23rd St., NW, Ste. 700
Washington, DC 20037
Phone: 202/466-1000

National Association of State Universities and Land-Grant Colleges
One DuPont Circle, NW, Ste. 710
Washington, DC 20036-1191
Phone: 202/778-0818

National Association of College and University Business Offices
One DuPont Circle, NW, Ste. 500
Washington, DC 20036
Phone: 202/861-2500

National Data Service for Higher Education
2400 Central Ave., B-2
Boulder, CO 80301
Phone: 800/444-8110.

The Center for Higher Education at Illinois State University conducts an annual survey of state appropriations to public institutions and publishes it in the *Grapevine*. Financial information on community colleges is available in the *Comparative Financial Data Survey of Public Community Colleges*, published by the National Association of College and University Business Officers (NACUBO). Finally, several states conduct more detailed cost studies on many public universities.

ANALYSIS

Cost analysis involves identification of the relevant resources and assignment of these resources to the units of output. Some costs are easily identified with a specific activity (e.g., a faculty member teaching a course). In other cases, it is impossible to associate a cost with a specific unit of output. In this situation you must distribute the costs to all the units of output. However, to be credible, your distribution must simulate the factors that influence cost.

We illustrate the steps in a cost analysis using as an example a fictitious anthropology department. Within each step, we discuss the decisions, data, and analyses activities required. As a starting point, we are seeking to answer three basic questions:

- *How much does it cost to teach anthropology?*
- *What is the cost of the anthropology program?*
- *How do our anthropology costs compare to peers?*

Figure 1

Induced Courseload Matrix

Student Credit Hour Distribution

Disciplines by Academic Level

		Anthro Lower Division	Anthro Upper Division	Anthro Grad Division	Geology Lower Division	Geology Upper Division	Geology Grad Division	Total SCH
Anthropology Degree Majors	Anthro Lower Division	700			300			1000
	Anthro Upper Division	150	700	100	75	400		1425
	Anthro Grad Division		175	300		50	75	600
	Total SCH	850	875	400	375	450	75	3025

STEP 1. *Identify the unit(s) of analysis.*

Our example centers on determining the costs of both anthropology instruction and the anthropology program. The units of analysis for anthropology instruction are anthropology course offerings. These courses usually are taught in a single academic department, but some disciplines do cross academic units. In our example, anthropology course offerings are taught only by the anthropology department. The result is expressed as a cost per student credit hour (SCH) of anthropology instruction.

An academic program is a mix of instructional offerings across academic units, and sometimes disciplines, which together meet the degree requirements of a program of study. Students register for courses within and outside the department of their major in completing program require-

ments. The units of analysis for an academic program are courses taken by anthropology majors. The result is expressed as an SCH cost per anthropology major.

Complexity increases when the unit of analysis is a program because you must determine the cost per course across all disciplines of courses taken by majors in a particular program. **Figure 1** illustrates the complexity of an anthropology program with only one other contributing discipline—geology. In this example, undergraduate and graduate anthropology students take courses in their own discipline as well as in geology. The anthropology program's total output, or load, in student credit hours is summarized in the total column.

Figure 1 utilizes an **induced courseload matrix** to identify the instructional load of a student on the institution. Most institutions look at the instructional load by department. However, an induced courseload matrix enables institutions to determine the instructional load for a particular group of students (e.g., anthropology majors). Applying the induced courseload matrix concept to even a small college requires computing support.

STEP 2. *Establish classification taxonomies.*

To make valid interinstitutional cost comparisons, the instructional offerings against which the costs are distributed must be uniform for each institution in the comparison. This is accomplished by aligning courses with disciplines rather than departments. The taxonomy used to accomplish this must be sufficiently broad to describe the myriad of disciplines and activities of postsecondary institutions. Most instructional cost studies use the CIP taxonomy to assign the units of output (e.g., courses) to disciplines.

Another similar taxonomy is needed to classify expenditures. In this case the expenditures must be disaggregated into a functional taxonomy. The taxonomy used most often to classify expenditures is part of the detailed procedures developed jointly by NCHEMS and NACUBO (1977) for determining the cost. The organizations identified eight primary functions for which colleges and universities budget resources: instruction, research, public service, academic support, student services, institutional support, operations and maintenance, and independent operation. Many institutions classify resources by these eight functions. In determining the instructional costs in the anthropology department, some resources designated for student services, academic support, institutional support, and operations and maintenance should be included.

STEP 3. *Define resource inputs.*

In a cost analysis, resource inputs are the resources committed to your unit of analysis. These resources are usually expressed as dollars. In some situations, inputs take other forms, such as faculty FTE or net assignable space. However, since dollars are the primary concern, it is rare when resources are expressed in other formats.

Before deciding which resource inputs are needed, answer these three questions:

- *Does your institution need budget or expenditure data?* The budget drives the academic plan of most institutions. As a result, budgeted cost per unit of output is sometimes more important than actual cost. This is especially true for public institutions where expenditure authority and the amount of appropriated resources are major concerns. If the institution is privately financed, or if budget shortfalls occur in public institutions, actual expenditures per unit of output are more important. Both budget and expenditure-based costs analyses have their place, and your analysis should focus on the most important to your institution.

- What *funds should be included?* Colleges and universities receive resources from four primary sources: (1) state/county/local governmental agencies, (2) tuition and fee collections, (3) self-generated revenues (e.g., inter-collegiate athletics, student activities), and (4) sponsored revenues. Your institution budgets and expends funds from each of these sources. If your institution is publicly financed, the relevant funding sources tend to be governmental subsidies. However, if your institution is private, tuition and fee collections and self-generated revenues are often included.

- *What is the time period?* Resources are budgeted and expended for a fixed period. The relevant period in private industry is a calendar or fiscal year. In postsecondary education, revenues and expenditures are summarized annually in the institution's financial statements. However, your analysis could be based on an academic term, academic year, or fiscal year. In our analysis of the instructional costs of the anthropology department, the focus is the academic year. However, we should also include the proportional fiscal year costs of activities, such as clerical support, used to support the academic year faculty.

STEP 4. *Select an output measure.*
Units of output are the measures against which your costs are distributed. There is no end to the list of possible units of output measures to relate to resource inputs. Students, faculty, employees, and space tend to be the workload measures around which resources are distributed. SCH or student FTE are used in studies of instructional cost. Student headcount is used in activities where the workload is driven by a student contact (e.g., advising, admissions, intramural sports). Many cost analyses focus on faculty or faculty FTE when analyzing the other primary programs of research and public service.

Most instructional cost analyses utilize cost per SCH, with separate measures by academic level: cost per SCH for lower division, upper division, graduate. Sometimes the cost per SCH is grouped into student FTE. For example, if the cost per SCH for graduate instruction is $250 and 10 graduate hours equal one student FTE, then the cost of an FTE graduate student is $2,500.

When student credit hours are the output measure, it is important that the assignment of credit to independent instruction is the same throughout the data. Institutions sometimes adopt assumptions relating independent instruction credits, such as dissertation or student teaching, to regular classroom credits (e.g., 12 credits of independent study equal one credit hour of traditional instruction). However, there is no universal standard in making this translation.

Figure 2

First-order Assignment of Faculty Effort to Departmental Activities

Anthropology Department Activities

	Instruction	Research	Public Service	Depart. Admin.	Inst. Admin.	Total
Faculty #1 Salary Distribution						
% of effort	40%	25%	5%	20%	10%	100%
Salary	$16,000	$10,000	$2,000	$8,000	$4,000	$40,000
All Faculty	(Faculty effort is averaged to obtain a department effort.)					
Average % of effort	60%	20%	10%	5%	5%	100%
Total Salaries	$208,539	$69,513	$34,757	$17,378	$17,378	$347,565

Using a common course numbering system across departments helps identify the courses with independent credits. When conducting interinstitutional comparisons, an agreed-upon method of converting nontraditional courses to the SCH equivalents of traditional courses is essential unless it is decided to exclude these courses from the analysis.

STEP 5. *Decide basis for assigning costs.*

Once you decide which resource inputs and units of output to include in your cost analysis, you must distribute the costs to the output. Costs are typically classified as either direct or indirect. **Direct costs** are those which are directly identifiable with an output measure. **Indirect costs** are associated with more than one activity (e.g., instruction and research) and must be distributed to each activity based on a cost assignment strategy. Almost all the costs are distributed in a first-order allocation to the various activities that constitute the total range of effort. After this distribution, the resources are distributed to the units of output in a second-order allocation.

Assigning department costs. In our example, the faculty in the anthropology department are involved in many activities. Our taxonomy classifies these activities as *instruction, research, public service, departmental administration,* and *institutional administration.* The task is to assign faculty effort to each activity based on an analysis of the time faculty spend on each activity.

Figure 2 is an example of the first-order assignment of faculty salaries to the various activities in the anthropology department. Since the purpose of our analysis is to determine the cost of anthropology instruction and the anthropology program, we allocate each faculty member's salary first to all the department's activities based on effort. In this example, $16,000 of the first faculty member's salary is allocated to instruction.

Once we have made our faculty assignment decisions, we must then assign nonfaculty departmental costs—both direct and indirect—to all the activities in the department. Nonfaculty direct costs are those easily identified

Figure 3		
Assignment of Anthropology Department Costs to Instruction		
Department Resource Inputs	First-order Assignment	Second-order Assignment to Instructional Subprograms (Lower, upper, graduate divisions)
Faculty salaries	$208,539	Student credit hours taught by subprogram
Administration	45,636	Student credit hours taught by subprogram
Advising	35,260	Number of students by subprogram
	$289,435	

with a specific activity, such as the cost of clerical support and supplies for instruction. Nonfaculty indirect costs usually are assumed to benefit all the department's activities proportionally, based on the distribution of faculty effort. For example, in **Figure 2**, 60 percent of all the faculty's effort in the department is in instruction. Therefore, 60 percent of the nonfaculty indirect costs would also be distributed to instruction.

After completing all first-order allocations, we then allocate the direct and indirect costs identified with instruction to the units of output in a second-order allocation. Departments frequently have three instructional subprograms—lower division, upper division, and graduate. Faculty direct costs in instruction can be assigned to each subprogram in several ways: (1) the student credit hours per course are divided by total student credit hours taught per faculty member, (2) the student contact hours per course are divided by total student contact hours per faculty member, or (3) the student credit hours per course, weighted by course level, are divided by total student credit hours per faculty member, also weighted by course level. (See NACUBO-NCHEMS [1977] for a complete discussion of assignment methods.)

Figure 3 illustrates the first- and second-order assignments of anthropology resources. In this example, $208,539 of faculty salaries are assigned to instruction. These resources are then assigned in a second-order allocation to lower division, upper division, and graduate instruction based on the course credit equivalents of the courses taught by each faculty members. We allocate $45,636 of departmental administrative costs to the instructional subprograms based on the student credit hours generated in each subprogram. The departmental administration costs include a portion of the chair's salary, clerical salaries, and nonfaculty salaries in the department.

	Figure 4			
	Cost per Student Credit Hour of Anthropology Instructional Subprograms			
Full Cost Resource Inputs	**Lower Division Costs**	**Upper Division Costs**	**Graduate Division Costs**	**Total Cost**
Department	$35,302	$122,719	$131,414	$289,435
Student Services	17,987	11,039	5,734	34,760
Academic Support	12,936	7,939	4,125	25,000
Institutional Support	25,873	20,003	4,124	50,000
Total Cost Allocated	$92,098	$161,275	$145,397	**$399,195**
Student Credit Hours	1,882	1,155	600	**3,637**
Cost per Credit Hour	$49	$140	$242	**$110**

Finally, we assign the entire $35,260 cost for student advisement to instruction. We distribute this amount to the three subprograms based on the number of students in each subprogram. This cost represents the salary of a full-time academic advisor in the department and the supplies allocated to the advising function.

Assigning college and institutional costs. College and institutional costs are expended on the eight primary functions of postsecondary education: instruction, research, public service, student services, academic support, institutional support, operations and maintenance, and independent operations. If your analysis is based on *full* costs, allocate an equitable portion of the college and institutional costs to your unit of analysis.

Resource inputs for student services benefit instruction. Some of these resources should be allocated to this activity. Resource inputs for academic support benefit instruction, research, and public service. Allocate these costs based on a method consistent with the activities at your institution. For example, you might base the allocation on the proportion of faculty FTE funded by instruction. If 90 percent of the faculty FTE at your institution are funded by instructional resources, allocate 90 percent of the academic support resources to that activity.

Follow a similar procedure in allocating the costs for the other functions: institutional support, operations and maintenance, and independent operations. Many institutions base these allocations on the relative size of the instruction, research, and public service budgets. For example, if instructional resources total $60 million, research $30 million, and public service $10 million, distribute these other costs in a 60-30-10 ratio.

Courses taken by Anthro Majors	SCH	x	Cost per SCH	=	Total Resources	
			Figure 5			
			Cost per Student Credit Hour			
			Undergraduate Anthropology Majors			
Lower Div Anthro	850	x	$49	=	$41,650	
Upper Div Anthro	700	x	$140	=	$98,000	
Lower Div Geo	375	x	$60	=	$22,500	
Upper Div Geo	400	x	$125	=	$50,000	**Program Cost per SCH**
	2,325				$212,150 =	**$91.25**

Once you allocate all the support resources to instruction, research, and public service, the first-order allocations are complete. Second-order allocation involves assigning these costs to instructional outputs. Many institutions make the second-order allocation based on the proportion of the institution's SCH weighted by academic level taught by the unit.

STEP 6. *Perform the analysis.*

Pulling all the information together, we are ready to answer the three original questions:

- *How much does it cost to teach anthropology?*
- *What is the cost of the anthropology program?*
- *How do our anthropology costs compare to peers?*

In our example, we allocated department resources to instruction in a first-order allocation based on the distribution of faculty effort. We based the second-order allocation of department costs on the three methods illustrated in **Figure 3.**

We first allocated college and institutional costs for student services, academic support, institutional support, operations and maintenance, and independent operations to instruction based on the proportional distribution of students, faculty, and budget. Second-order allocations involved further distribution by academic level.

Figure 4 summarizes all costs allocated to the instruction of anthropology. Dividing the costs by the student credit hours at each academic level yields a lower division cost of $49 per SCH, an upper division cost of $140, and a graduate cost of $242. This answers the first question: *How much does it cost to teach anthropology?*

Determining the cost of the anthropology program is based on the induced courseload matrix analysis presented earlier in **Figure 1**. To calculate the total cost of the anthropology program, we would need to combine the costs per SCH determined in the analysis above with a similar analysis for the geology department.

Figure 5 illustrates this calculation. In this example, we multiply the lower division stu-

137

Figure 6			
Interinstitutional Comparison of the Cost per SCH			
Instructional Level	**Your Institution**	**Institution A**	**Institution B**
Lower Division	$49	$59	$75
Upper Division	$140	$110	$90
Graduate	$242	$225	$175

dent credit hours generated by anthropology majors taking anthropology and geology courses by the cost per SCH for instruction in these disciplines. We followed the same process with upper division credit hours. We then added all the resources together and divided by the total SCH. The result is an average cost per SCH for anthropology majors—$91.25 per unit.

It is easy to see how difficult this becomes if students are taking courses in many disciplines. A variation of this measure is to convert the cost per SCH to student FTE. For example, if lower division FTE are based on 15 SCH and upper division on 12 SCH, the cost of one full-time anthropology major is $1,224. This answers the second question: *What is the cost of the anthropology program?*

How do our costs compare? Interinstitutional cost comparisons are difficult because of the potential for noncomparability in the data and methods used to calculate per unit cost. The best advice for public institutions in making interinstitutional cost comparisons is to use comparator institutions within your own state or system.

The reason is simple: standard definitions, data collection, and costing methods free you to concentrate on the functional differences between institutions. Also, it helps to compare departments of comparable size so differences in economies of scale are not a problem.

Assuming that the peer institutions have comparable costing procedures in place, **Figure 6** illustrates how anthropology costs at three institutions differ. This answers the last question: *How do our anthropology costs compare to peers?*

COMMUNICATION

In deciding how to best communicate the results of your cost analysis, keep in mind that cost comparisons are sensitive and controversial. First drafts of reports are rarely final drafts. Show others your early drafts and back-up material before committing to a format or set of conclusions. Given the politics of cost analysis, carefully weigh who sees these early drafts. You do not want your tentative conclusions to be the topic of conversation before your primary audience receives the report.

Staff in your own office are the best candidates for this task. However, given the nature of cost analysis, there are occasions when reviews are best performed by individuals outside the institution.

When presenting and distributing the cost analysis, keep in mind that these studies tend to draw the attention of the press. Have a press release or statement ready if needed.

REMEMBER

Remember that the best cost analysis is only an estimate of the actual cost. How good an estimate is depends on how closely the methods selected to distribute costs to the units of output simulate the actual consumption of resources. Therefore, any cost analysis should be interpreted in orders of magnitude.

When making interinstitutional cost comparisons, try to understand the functional differences between your institution and the comparator institutions. Collect as much nonfinancial, policy, and demographic data as possible on the comparator schools. Whenever possible, select comparator institutions from your own state or system, since these institutions are financed in a manner similar to yours. Finally, aggregate data at the highest level possible. As the level of aggregation increases, so does the comparability of the data.

We expect to see a resurgence of cost analysis as a result of the large number of institutions experiencing financial difficulty. In this environment, cost analysis is an effective tool in making resource allocation and reallocation decisions.